THE
ETHERIC
DOUBLE
The Health Aura of Man

THE
ETHERIC
DOUBLE

The Health Aura of Man
A.E. POWELL

*This publication made possible with
the assistance of the Kern Foundation*

The Theosophical Publishing House
Wheaton, Ill. U.S.A.
Madras, India/London, England

Fifth Quest book printing 1987

Original Quest Book edition 1969. Published by The
Theosophical Publishing House, a department of The
Theosophical Society in America. Published by arrangement
with The Theosophical Publishing House Ltd., London.

ISBN: 0-8356-0075-0

Printed in the United States of America

THIS BOOK IS DEDICATED
WITH GRATITUDE AND APPRECIATION
TO ALL THOSE
WHO HAVE PROVIDED THE MATERIALS
OUT OF WHICH
IT HAS BEEN FASHIONED

TABLE OF CONTENTS

LIST OF DIAGRAMS

AUTHORITIES QUOTED

Ancient Wisdom . . .	Annie Besant .	1897	*A W*
Astral Plane	C. W. Leadbeater	1910	*A P*
Changing World. . . .	Annie Besant .	1909	*C W*
Clairvoyance	C. W. Leadbeater	1908	*Cl*
Death and After. . . .	Annie Besant .	1901	*D A*
Dreams	C. W. Leadbeater	1903	*D*
Experiments in Psychical Science	W. J. Crawford	1919	*E P S*
First Principles of Theosophy .	C. Jinarajadasa	1921	*F P T*
Five Years of Theosophy .	H. P. Blavatsky	1910	*F Y T*
Hidden Side of Things, Vol. I. .	C. W. Leadbeater	1913	*H S,* I
Hidden Side of Things, Vol. II. .	C. W. Leadbeater	1913	*H S,* II
Human Atmosphere . .	W. J. Kilner .	1911	*H A*
Inner Life, Vol. I. . .	C. W. Leadbeater	1910	*I L,* I
Inner Life, Vol. II. . .	C. W. Leadbeater	1911	*I L,* II
Introduction to Yoga . .	Annie Besant .	1908	*Y*
Invisible Helpers . . .	C. W. Leadbeater	1908	*I H*
Ladder of Lives . . .	Annie Besant .	1908 ?	*L L*
Life After Death . .	C. W. Leadbeater	1912	*L A D*
Man and his Bodies . .	Annie Besant .	1900	*M B*
Man, Visible and Invisible .	C. W. Leadbeater	1902	*M V*
Man, Whence, How and Whither .	Annie Besant and C. W. Leadbeater .	1913	*M W H W*
Monad	C. W. Leadbeater	1920	*M*
Nature's Finer Forces. .	Rama Prasad .	1897	*N F F*
Nature's Mysteries . .	A. P. Sinnett .	1901	*N M*
Other Side of Death . .	C. W. Leadbeater	1904	*O S D*
Phenomena of Materialisation .	Von Schrenck Notzing .	1920	*P M*
Psychic Structures . .	W. J. Crawford	1921	*P S*
Rationale of Mesmerism .	A. P. Sinnett .	1902	*R M*
Reality of Psychic Phenomena .	W. J. Crawford	1919	*R P P*
Science of the Sacraments .	C. W. Leadbeater	1920	*S O S*
Secret Doctrine, Vol. I. .	H. P. Blavatsky	1905	*S D,* I
Secret Doctrine, Vol. II. .	H. P. Blavatsky	1905	*S D,* II
Self and Its Sheaths . .	Annie Besant .	1903	*S S*
Seven Principles of Man .	Annie Besant .	1904	*S P*
Some Glimpses of Occultism .	C. W. Leadbeater	1909	*S G O*
Study in Consciousness .	Annie Besant .	1904	*S C*
Textbook of Theosophy .	C. W. Leadbeater	1912	*T B T*
Theosophy	Annie Besant .	1909	*T*
Theosophy and the New Psychology	Annie Besant .	1909	*T N P*
Thought Power . . .	Annie Besant .	1903	*T P*

PUBLISHER'S PREFACE

THE author's aim in compiling the books in this series was to save students much time and labour by providing a condensed synthesis of the considerable literature on the respective subjects of each volume, coming mostly from the pens of Annie Besant and C. W. Leadbeater. The accompanying list shows the large number of books from which he drew. So far as possible, the method adopted was to explain the form side first, before the life side: to describe the objective mechanism of phenomena and then the activities of consciousness that are expressed through the mechanism. There is no attempt to prove or even justify any of the statements. Marginal references give opportunity to refer to the sources.

The works of H. P. Blavatsky were not used because the author said that the necessary research in *The Secret Doctrine* and other writings would have been too vast a task for him to undertake. He added: "The debt to H. P. Blavatsky is greater than could ever be indicated by quotations from her monumental volumes. Had she not shown the way in the first instance, later investigators might never have found the trail at all."

FOREWORD

by members of the Science Group of the
Theosophical Research Centre, London, England

The Etheric Double was first published in 1925 as one of a series by the same author dealing with the inner structure of Man. It is now re-presented to the public unchanged except for the omission from the last chapter of a reference to local research, active when the book was written.

No attempt has been made to augment or otherwise bring up to date this classic in the light of understanding accumulated during the intervening forty-odd years. As A. E. Powell said himself in his introduction, this is a compilation from forty main works published between 1897 and 1921 and in view of their wide range and the painstaking thoroughness with which they were extracted, the collated information may fairly be taken to summarise the general views upon the subject *up to* 1925.

In more recent years, a better appreciation has been built up of the way the unconscious mind functions, and sources of possible error have been discerned in the operation of mediumistic faculties which necessitate caution concerning information obtained through their use. Much of the contents of *The Etheric Double* is derived from the exercise of clair-sentience (or extrasensory perception, as it is now called) and although the contents may be accurate, there is as yet no accepted method of confirming them. This is not to cast doubt on the honesty of those who recorded the observations; they were persons of unimpeachable integrity who continually emphasised their pioneering status and fallibility. There is no doubt that the psychic phenomena they described were experienced by them and, indeed, others have since confirmed some of their accounts. The sources of possible error referred to lie one stage deeper than that —in the psychic mechanisms for experiencing what they did. This is the still unresolved and fascinating province of parapsychology.

Further assistance can be expected towards corroborating or refuting the observations and the theory of the etheric double from data emerging in the natural sciences, but at present there are few points of contact. Space craft have taken recording instruments to Mars and Venus, and electron microscopes in common laboratory service provide enormous magnifications of what is normally invisible, but there is hardly any information relating to etheric states of matter that has been acquired in a similar direct and orthodox way. Work with recording devices has so far failed to detect etheric matter in its normal working state and thereby confirm it as physical or near-physical substance. Probably the closest approach has been in studies of ectoplasm, which seems to be the temporary and abnormal condition of a plastic and extrudable component of the human body that becomes amenable to test only when it has been made external and densified into tangible form by the special and unconsciously exercised psychic abilities of certain rare people. When the densification ceases and the material is withdrawn again into the donor's body, it could well be returning to its function as part of a less easily identified etheric constitution. However, much more work is needed before this can be concluded with any confidence.

Since rigorously established evidence can still neither confirm nor deny, it is reasonable to hold the theory and information presented here as a hypothesis for further investigation. This is the procedure in all scientific work and, in fact, little progress can be made without some tentative working concept as context and guide. But it is essential to remember that an adopted hypothesis may have to be modified or even rejected as the work proceeds, and this is most likely during the early stages of an exploration. It happens frequently in the natural sciences of the physical world for which our ordinary language and mathematical symbology are expressly designed. How much more likely must this be in a domain more psychic than physical.

Modern investigators continue the quest for a deeper understanding of Man's nature and constitution and they have noted the more recent developments in psychology and parapsychology that underlie the caution sounded here. However, their gratitude is due to Powell for his orderly presentation of statements and ideas current in 1925; time and effort need not now be spent on the reference material that he so ably examined for them. Here is ample justification for reprinting his work just as he wrote it.

The Science Group,
Theosophical Research Centre,
London, England

1968   H. TUDOR EDMUNDS, *Chairman*

INTRODUCTION

THIS book has been compiled with the object of presenting to the student of Occultism a coherent synthesis of all, or nearly all, the information regarding the Etheric Double, and other closely allied phenomena, which has been given to the world through the medium of modern Theosophical and psychical research literature.

This information is scattered over a very large number of books and articles, some forty of which the compiler has consulted, a list of these being given on page ix. The writer wishes it understood that his work is a compilation—nothing more. All he has done is to collect and arrange the material which others have provided.

There are many advantages in this method of study. In these busy days few have the leisure, even if they possess the inclination, to search through some scores of books for scattered items of knowledge, and then to weld them into a coherent whole. It is better, therefore, for one to do this work, that others may benefit and save their own time and labour. The work of the compiler brings to light many new relationships between fragments culled from divers sources, and under his hand the mosaic gradually forms itself into a pattern. His work, necessarily intensive, recalls to notice many isolated and often forgotten facts, which may be of little value or interest considered individually, but which collectively constitute a substantial and useful array. Finally, the picture which the compiler presents not only displays in orderly fashion what is known to-day, but, by its very orderliness, reveals where our knowledge is incomplete. Recognising such gaps in our knowledge, other investigators may perhaps turn their attention in those directions and so make the picture more nearly complete.

The compiler has throughout used his best endeavour to present the material he has gathered with scrupulous exactitude. In very many cases he has employed the actual words, adapted or abridged where necessary to the context, of the authors he has consulted ; but, not to make the text burdensome and unsightly with large numbers of inverted commas, these have been consistently omitted. In order, however, that students may, if they wish, refer to the original sources of information, the references have been provided, in abbreviated form, in the margin of the text.

The compiler would be grateful to any students who would call his attention (1) to any inaccuracies in his work ; (2) to any omissions of material which he may have overlooked.

The diagrams and charts contained in the text are original ; they are intended to be purely diagrammatic, and in no sense pictures of the actual phenomena they attempt to illustrate

A. E. P.

THE ETHERIC DOUBLE

CHAPTER I

GENERAL DESCRIPTION

EVERY student of Occultism is familiar with the fact that man possesses several bodies or vehicles through which he is enabled to express himself on the various planes of nature—physical, astral, mental, and so forth.

The occultist finds that physical matter exists in seven grades or orders of density, viz. :

> Atomic.
> Sub-Atomic.
> Super-Etheric.
> Etheric.
> Gaseous.
> Liquid.
> Solid.

Particles of all these grades enter into the composition of the physical vehicle. The latter, however, has two well-marked divisions, viz., the dense body, composed of solids, liquids and gases, and the Etheric Body, or Double, as it is frequently called, consisting of the four finer grades of physical matter. *M B* 28.

It will be our purpose in these chapters to study this Etheric Double : its nature, appearance, functions, its relationships to the other vehicles, its connection with Prâna, or Vitality, its birth, growth and decay, its connection with certain methods of healing, with mesmerism, with mediumship and materialisations, the powers it can be made to exercise, and a host of miscellaneous etheric phenomena with which it is connected.

Briefly, we shall find that the Etheric Double, while necessary to the life of the physical body, is not, properly speaking, a separate vehicle of consciousness : that it receives and distributes the vital force which emanates from the sun and is thus intimately connected with the physical health : that it possesses certain Chakrams or Force-Centres of its own, each with its distinct function : that upon the action of etheric matter mainly depends the memory of the dream life : that it plays an important part in determining the kind of physical vehicle which an incarnating ego will receive : that, like the physical body, it dies and decays in due course, releasing the " soul " for the next stage in its cyclic journey : that it is especially associated with what is known as Vital or Magnetic Healing, and also with Mesmerism, whether for purposes of healing, anæsthesia, or trance : that it is the principal factor concerned in séance-room phenomena, such as the movement of objects, production of " raps " and other sounds, and materialisations of all kinds : that the development of etheric faculties confers new powers and reveals many etheric phenomena, which are beyond the experience of most men : that by the use of the matter of the etheric body objects may be " magnetised," much as living beings may be mesmerised : and, finally, that the etheric body provides the material out of which the substance known as ectoplasm is formed.

The Etheric Double has been given a variety of names. In early Theosophical literature it was often called the astral body, the astral man, or the Linga Sharîra. In all later writings, however, none of these terms are ever applied to the Etheric Double, as they belong properly to the body composed of astral matter, the body of Kâma of the Hindus. In reading the Secret Doctrine, therefore, and other books of the older literature, the student must be on his guard not to confuse the two quite distinct bodies, known to-day as the Etheric Double and the Astral Body.

The correct Hindu name for the Etheric Double is

S S 58.

A W 231;
S D I 181.

A W 231;

Prânamâyakosha, or vehicle of Prâna : in German it is *S S* 57.
known as the "Doppelgänger" : after death, when *S P* 8.
separated from the dense physical body, it is known as
the "wraith," and has also been called the "phantom,"
"apparition," or "churchyard ghost." In Râja Yoga *S S* 63.
the Etheric Double and the dense body together are
known as the Sthûlopâdhi, or lowest Upâdhi of
Âtmâ.

Every solid, liquid and gaseous particle of the *M B* 28.
physical body is surrounded with an etheric envelope :
hence the Etheric Double, as its name implies, is a
perfect duplicate of the dense form. In size it projects
about one quarter of an inch beyond the skin. The
etheric aura, however, or Health Aura as it is frequently
called, projects normally several inches beyond the
skin : this will be further described later.

It is important to notice that the dense body and
the Etheric Double vary together as to their quality :
hence one who sets himself deliberately to purify his
dense body, at the same time automatically refines its
etheric counterpart.

Into the composition of the Etheric Double must *A P* 22.
enter something of all the different grades of etheric
matter, but the proportions may vary greatly, and are
determined by several factors, such as the race, sub-
race, and type of a man, as well as by his individual
karma.

As yet, the only information which the compiler has
been able to gather regarding the particular properties
and functions of each of the four grades of etheric
matter is the following :—

1. Etheric : The medium of ordinary current *L L* 6.
electricity, and of sound.
2. Super-Etheric : The medium of light.
3. Sub-Atomic : The medium of " the finer forms
of electricity."
4. Atomic : The medium for the transmission of thought from brain to
brain.

The following is stated, in *Theosophy* for May, 1922, by F. T. Peirce, to be probably correct :—

Occult Chemistry.	Physics.	Example.
E_1 Atomic.	Electronic.	Electron.
E_2 Sub-atomic.	Positive nucleus.	Alpha particle.
E_3 Super-etheric.	Neutralised nucleus.	Neutron.
E_4 Etheric	Atomic.	Nascent N.
		Atomic H.
Gaseous.	Molecular gas, etc.	H_2, N_2 or gaseous compounds.

M V 128.

In appearance the Etheric Double is a pale violet-grey or blue-grey, faintly luminous, and coarse or fine

M B 28.

in texture according as the dense physical body is coarse or fine.

M B 29;
A W 63;
T B T 87.

The Etheric Double has two main functions. Firstly, it absorbs Prâna, or Vitality, and distributes this to the whole physical body, as we shall see in detail presently.

Secondly, it acts as an intermediary or bridge between the dense physical body and the astral body, transmitting the consciousness of physical sense-con-

S S 63.

tacts through the etheric brain to the astral body, and also transmitting consciousness from the astral and higher levels down into the physical brain and nervous system.

In addition, the Etheric Double develops within itself certain Centres by means of which the man is able to cognise the etheric world and its hosts of etheric phenomena. These powers or faculties will also be described in due course.

It is important to recognise that the Etheric Double, being merely a part of the physical body, is not normally capable of acting as a separate vehicle of consciousness,

S P 11.

in which a man can live or function. It has only a diffused consciousness belonging to its parts, and has no mentality, nor does it readily serve as a medium of mentality, when disjoined from the dense counterpart. As it is a vehicle, not of mental consciousness, but of Prâna or Vitality, its dislocation from the dense par-

ticles to which it conveys the life-currents is disturbing
and unhealthy. In normal, healthy persons, in fact, *A W* 292.
the separation of the Etheric Double from the dense
body is a matter of difficulty, and the Double is *S P* 8.
unable to move away from the body to which it
belongs.

In persons known as physical or materialising
mediums the Double is comparatively easily detachable,
and its etheric matter forms the basis of many phenomena of materialisation, which will be dealt with more
fully in a later chapter.

The Double may be separated from the dense physical
body by accident, death, anæsthetics, such as ether or
gas, or mesmerism. The Double being the connecting
link between the brain and the higher consciousness,
the forcible extrusion of it from the dense physical body
by anæsthetics necessarily produces anæsthesia.

Further than this, the etheric matter thus forced out
usually wraps itself round the astral body and dulls the
consciousness of that vehicle also : hence after the *H S I* 342.
effects of the anæsthetics have worn off there is usually
no memory in the brain consciousness of the time spent
in the astral vehicle.

The method and consequences of withdrawal of
etheric matter by mesmerism will be dealt with more
fully in the chapter specially devoted to the purpose.

In conditions of weak health or nervous excitement
the Etheric Double may also in great part be extruded
from its dense counterpart : the latter then becomes *A W* 70.
very dully conscious, or entranced, according to the
lesser or greater amount of the etheric matter extruded.

Separation of the Double from the dense body is
generally accompanied by a considerable decrease of
vitality in the latter, the double becoming more
vitalised as the energy in the dense body diminishes.
In *Posthumous Humanity* Colonel H. S. Olcott *S P* 9.
says :—

" When the double is projected by a trained expert,
even the body seems torpid, and the mind in a ' brown
study ' or dazed state ; the eyes are lifeless in expression,

the heart and lung actions feeble and often the temperature much lowered. It is very dangerous to make any sudden noise or burst into the room under such circumstances ; for, the double being by instantaneous reaction drawn back into the body, the heart convulsively palpitates, and death even may be caused."

S P 9.

So intimate, in fact, is the connection between the etheric and the dense bodies that an injury inflicted on the Etheric Double will appear as a lesion on the dense body, this being an instance of the curious phenomenon known as repercussion. It is well known that repercussion can also occur in the case of the astral body, an injury to the latter, under certain circumstances, reproducing itself in the physical body.

I H 54–5.

It seems probable, however, that repercussion can occur only in the case of perfect materialisation, where the form is both visible and tangible, and not when it is (1) tangible though not visible, or (2) visible though not tangible.

I H 57.

It must be borne in mind that the above applies only where matter of the Etheric Double is used for the materialised form. When the materialisation is formed of matter from the circumambient ether, an injury to the form could affect the physical body by repercussion no more than an injury to a marble statue could injure the man himself.

D 13.

It must also be borne in mind that etheric matter, though invisible to ordinary sight, is still purely physical, and can therefore be affected by cold and heat,

H S I 449.
S P 10.

and also by powerful acids.

Persons who have lost a limb by amputation sometimes complain that they can feel pain at the extremities of the amputated limb, *i.e.*, at the place where the limb used to be.

This is due to the fact that the etheric portion of the limb is not removed with the dense physical portion, but can still be seen in its place by clairvoyant sight, and therefore, under suitable stimulus, sensations can be aroused in this etheric limb and transmitted to the consciousness.

There are a large number of other phenomena connected with the Etheric Double, its extrusion from the dense body, its emanations, and so forth, but these can be dealt with more conveniently and satisfactorily at a later stage, after we have studied the nature and methods of working of Prâna, or Vitality.

CHAPTER II

PRÂNA, OR VITALITY

(See Diagrams I., II. (1), (2), (3), (4))

H S I 64.
I L I 461.

IT is known to occultists that there are at least three separate and distinct forces which emanate from the sun and reach our planet. There may be countless other forces, for all we know to the contrary, but at any rate we know of these three. They are :—

1. Fohat, or Electricity.
2. Prâna, or Vitality.
3. Kundalini, or Serpent-Fire.

Fohat, or Electricity, comprises practically all the physical forces of which we know, all of which are convertible into one another, such as electricity, magnetism, light, heat, sound, chemical affinity, motion, and so forth.

Prâna, or Vitality, is a vital force, the existence of which is not yet formally recognised by orthodox Western scientists, though probably a few of them suspect it.

Kundalini, or Serpent-Fire, is a force known as yet only to very few. It is entirely unknown and unsuspected by orthodox Western science.

These three forces remain distinct, and none of them can at this level be converted into either of the others. This is a point of great importance, which the student should clearly grasp.

Further, these three forces have no connection with the Three Great Outpourings ; * the Outpourings are definite efforts made by the Solar Deity. Fohat, Prâna and Kundalini, on the other hand, seem rather the results of His life, His qualities in manifestation without any visible effort.

* *Vide* note on p. 21.

DIAGRAM I
SOLAR FORCES

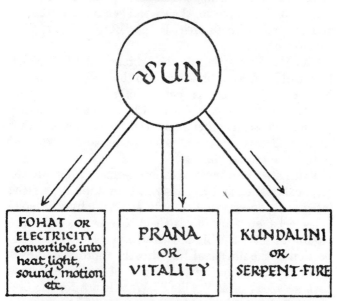

Each of these manifests on all planes of the Solar System.

Prâna is a Sanskrit word, derived from *pra*, forth, and *an*, to breathe, move, live. Thus *pra-an*, Prâna, means to breathe forth, life-breath or life-energy being the nearest English equivalents of the Sanskrit term. As, in Hindu thought, there is but one Life, one Consciousness, Prâna has been used for the Supreme Self, the energy of the One, the Life of the Logos. Hence, Life on each plane may be spoken of as the Prâna of the plane, Prâna becoming the life-breath in every creature. *S C* 155-6.

"I am Prâna . . . Prâna is life," says Indra, the great Deva who stands as the Head of the hierarchy of life in the lower world. Prâna here clearly means the totality of the life-forces. In the Mundakopanishat it is stated that from Brahman the One comes Prâna—or Life. Prâna is also described as Âtmâ in its outgoing activity : " From Âtmâ this Prâna is born " (Prashnopanishat). Shankara says that Prâna is Kriyâshakti— *S S* 57. *Y* 13-4. *S S* 40-1. *S S* 57.

the shakti of doing, not of knowing. It is classed as one
of the seven Elements, which correspond to the seven
regions of the universe, the seven sheaths of Brahman,
S S 41. and so forth. These are : Prâna, Manas, Ether, Fire,
Air, Water, Earth.

S P 14. The Hebrews speak of the " breath of life," which
they call Nephesch, breathed into the nostrils of Adam.
Nephesch, however, is not strictly speaking Prâna
alone, but Prâna combined with the next principle,
S D I 262-3. Kâma. These together make the " vital spark " that
is the " Breath of life in man, in beast or insect, of
physical, material life."

D A 12. Translated into more Western terms, Prâna, on the
physical plane, is best described as Vitality, as the
integrating energy that co-ordinates the physical molecules, cells, etc., and holds them together as a definite
organism. It is the life-breath within the organism, the
portion of the universal Life-Breath, appropriated by a
given organism during the period of bodily existence
that we speak of as " a life." Were it not for the presence of Prâna, there could be no physical body as an
integral whole, working as one entity ; without Prâna
the body would be nothing more than a collection of
S S 58. independent cells. Prâna links up and connects these
into one complex whole, playing along the branches
S C 91-2. and meshes of the " life-web," that shimmering golden
web of inconceivable fineness and delicate beauty,
formed out of a single thread of buddhic matter, a pro-
longation of the Sûtrâtmâ, within the meshes of which
the coarser atoms are built together.

H S I 68. Prâna is absorbed by all living organisms, a sufficient
supply of it seeming to be a necessity of their existence.
S D I 586-7. It is not, therefore, in any sense a product of life, but
the living animal, plant, etc., are its products. Too
great an exuberance of it in the nervous system may
lead to disease and death, just as too little leads to
exhaustion and ultimately death.

S D I I 627. H. P. Blavatsky compares Prâna, the active power
producing all *vital* phenomena, to oxygen, the supporter
of combustion, the life-giving gas, the active *chemical*

agent in all organic life. A comparison is also drawn between the Etheric Double, the inert vehicle of life, and nitrogen, an inert gas with which oxygen is mixed to adapt the latter for animal respiration, and which also enters largely into all organic substances.

The fact that the cat is pre-eminently endowed with prâna has given rise to the popular idea of the cat having " nine lives," and appears to have been indirectly connected with the reasons for this animal being regarded in Egypt as sacred.

S D I I 583.

On the physical plane prâna builds up all minerals, and is the controlling agent in the chemico-physiological changes in protoplasm, which lead to differentiation and the building of the various tissues of the bodies of plants, animals and men. They show its presence by the power of responding to stimuli.

S C 157-8.

The blending of astral with physical prâna creates nerve-matter, which is fundamentally the cell, and which gives the power to feel pleasure and pain. The cells develop into fibres, as the result of thought, the prâna pulsating along those fibres being composed of physical, astral and mental prâna.

Within the physical plane atoms themselves, the prâna courses along the spirillæ. In our Chain, in the First Round, the Monadic Life, flowing through the Spiritual Triad (Atmâ-Buddhi-Manas), vivifies the first set of spirillæ, and these are used by the prânic currents which affect the dense physical body. In the Second Round, the Monad vivifies the second set of spirillæ, and through them runs the prâna connected with the Etheric Double. In the Third Round, the third set of spirillæ is awakened by the Monadic life, and through them courses the kâmic prâna, which makes sensation of pleasure and pain possible. In the Fourth Round, the Monadic life awakens the fourth set of spirillæ, which become the vehicle for the kâma-manasic prâna, thus making the atoms fit to be built into a brain for thought.

S C 111-3.

This is as far as normal humanity has progressed. Certain yoga practices (in the use of which great caution is required, lest injury should be inflicted on the brain) bring about the development of the fifth and sixth sets of spirillæ, which serve as channels for higher forms of consciousness.

O C 22-3.

The seven spirillæ in the atom must not be confused with the " whorls," of which there are ten, three coarser and seven finer. In the three coarser whorls flow currents of different electricities, whilst the seven finer whorls respond to etheric waves of all kinds—sound, light, heat, etc.

S P 15.
S D I 245 &
269.

The *Secret Doctrine* speaks of Prâna as the "invisible" or "fiery" lives which supply the microbes with "vital constructive energy," thus enabling them to build the physical cells, the size of the smallest bacterium relatively to that of a "fiery life" being as that of an elephant to the tiniest infusoria. "Every visible thing in this universe was built by such lives, from conscious and divine primordial man, down to the unconscious

F Y T 255.

agents that construct matter." "By the manifestation of Prâna, the spirit which is speechless appears as the speaker."

The whole of constructive vitality, in the universe and in man, is thus summed up as Prâna.

S C 152-3,
note.

An atom is also a "life," but the consciousness is that of the Third Logos. A microbe is a "life," the consciousness being that of the Second Logos, appropriated and modified by the Planetary Logos and the "Spirit of the Earth."

S D I 579-
81.

The *Secret Doctrine* also speaks of a "fundamental dogma" of occult science, that the Sun is the storehouse of Vital Force, and that from the sun issue those life-currents which thrill through space, as through the organisms of every living thing on earth. Paracelsus thus referred to Prâna : "The whole of the Microcosm is potentially contained in the Liquor Vitæ, a nerve fluid . . . in which is contained the nature, quality, character, and essence of all beings." Paracelsus also

S D I 591.

spoke of it as the Archæus. Dr. B. Richardson, F.R.S., wrote of it as "nervous ether." The Nasmyth willow leaves are the reservoirs of the solar vital energy, the

real sun being hidden behind the visible sun, and
generating the vital fluid, which circulates throughout
our System in a ten-year cycle.

The old Aryan sang that Surya "hiding behind his
Yogi, robes his head that no one could see." *F Y T* 162.

The dress of Indian ascetics is dyed a red-yellow
hue, with pinkish patches on it, and is intended
rudely to represent the prâna in men's blood, the
symbol of the vital principle in the sun, or what is
now called the chromosphere, the "rose-coloured"
region.

The nerve-centres themselves are of course provided *S S* 55-6.
by the "food-sheath" or dense body, but Prâna is the
controlling energy which acts through the nerve-centres,
making the food-sheath obedient, and fashioning it for
the purpose which the I, seated in the higher intelligence, demands.

It is important to note that although the nerves are
in the physical body, it is not the physical body, as
such, which has the power of feeling. As a sheath, the
physical body does not feel : it is a receiver of impressions only. The outer body receives the impact, but
in its own cells does not lie the power of feeling pleasure
or pain, except in a very vague, dull and "massive"
way, giving rise to vague, diffused feelings, such as
those of general fatigue, for example.

The physical contacts are transmitted inwards by
prâna, and these are acute, sharp, keen, specific, quite
different from the heavy, diffused sensations deriving
from the cells themselves. It is thus in every case *S S* 59.
prâna which gives the sense-activity to the physical
organs, and which transmits the outer vibration to the
sense-centres, which are situated in kâma, in the
sheath which is next to that of prâna, the Manomaya-
kosha. It is by means of the Etheric Double that
prâna runs along the nerves of the body and thus
enables them to act not only as the carriers of external
impacts but also of motor force, originated from *M B* 29.
within.

It is the play of the prânic life-currents in the Etheric *A W* 87-88.

Doubles of minerals, vegetables and animals which awaken out of latency the astral matter involved in the structure of their atomic and molecular constituents, thus producing a " thrill " which enables the Monad of form to draw in astral materials, which are built by nature-spirits into a loosely constituted mass, the future astral body.

S C 149–50.   In the mineral, astral matter is so little active that there is no perceptible working from the astral to the physical. In the higher plants the increased astral activity affects their etheric and, through this, their dense matter. With animals, the much greater astral consciousness affects their Etheric Doubles and, by these etheric vibrations, the building of the nervous system, which was dimly foreshadowed only in plants, is stimulated.

S C 153–4.   It is, thus, impulses set up by consciousness—*willing* to experience—which cause astral vibrations, these producing vibrations in etheric matter : the impulse thus comes from the consciousness, but the actual building of the nervous system, which the consciousness at this stage is unable to undertake, is performed by etheric nature-spirits, directed by the Shining Ones of the Third Elemental Kingdom and the Logos working through the Group Soul.

S C 160–1.   There appears first in the astral body a centre, having the function of receiving and responding to vibrations from outside. From this centre, vibrations pass to the etheric body, causing there etheric vortices which draw into themselves dense physical particles : these eventually form a nerve-cell, and groups of cells, which, receiving vibrations from the outer physical world, transmit them back to the astral centres, the physical and astral centres thus acting and reacting on one another, each in consequence becoming more complicated and more effective. Out of these nerve-cells the sympathetic system is built first, by impulses, as we have seen, originating in the *astral* world : later the cerebro-spinal system is constructed, by impulses originating in the *mental* world.

The sympathetic system always remains directly
connected with the astral centres; but it is important
to note that these astral centres *are not the astral
chakrams*, of which we shall speak later, but are merely
aggregations in the astral sheath which form the
beginnings of the centres which will build the organs
in the physical body. The astral chakrams are not
formed till a much later period in evolution. — *S C* 164-7.

From these centres then—which are *not* the chakrams
—ten organs in the physical are formed : five to receive
impressions, Jñânendriyas, " knowledge-senses," or
sense-centres in the brain, which eventually are connected with eyes, ears, tongue, nose and skin : and five
to convey vibrations from consciousness to the outer
world, Karmendriyas, " action-senses," or sense-centres
which cause action, these being the motor-centres in
the brain, to be connected with the sense-organs in
hands, feet, larynx, organs of generation and excretion.

The student must carefully note that the *prâna*
which courses along the nerves is quite separate and
distinct from what is called a man's *magnetism*, or
nerve-fluid, which is generated within his own body.
This *nerve-fluid* or magnetism keeps the etheric matter
circulating along the nerves, or, more accurately, along — *S G O* 159.
a coating of ether which surrounds each nerve, much as
the blood circulates through the veins. And just as — *H S I* 81.
the blood carries oxygen to the body, so does the nerve-
fluid convey prâna.

Furthermore, just as the particles of the dense
physical body are constantly changing and being
replaced by fresh particles derived from food, water and
air, so are the particles of the etheric body being constantly changed and replaced by fresh etheric particles,
these being taken into the body along with the food
eaten, with the air breathed, and with prâna, in the
form known as the Vitality Globule, as will presently be
described.

Prâna, or vitality, exists on all the planes—physical, — *H S I* 64.
astral, mental, etc. Prâna, the One Life, is " the nave — *F Y T* 123.
to which are attached the *seven* spokes of the universal

c

wheel " (*Hymn to Prâna, Atharva Veda*, XI., 4). We
are here, however, concerned only with its appearance
and methods of work in the lowest, the physical plane.

I L I 444.   It must also be noted that prâna on the physical
plane is seven-fold, *i.e.*, there are seven varieties of it.

H S I 64.   We have seen already that prâna is quite separate
and distinct from light, heat, etc., but nevertheless its

DIAGRAM II
THE VITALITY GLOBULE
(1) An Ultimate Physical Atom

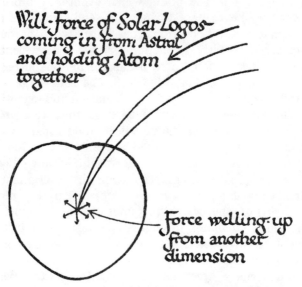

Will-Force of Solar Logos
coming in from Astral
and holding Atom
together

Force welling-up
from another
dimension

For details of atom, see *Occult Chemistry*, Plate II., and page 5, *et seqq.*

manifestation on the physical plane appears to depend
upon sunlight : for when sunlight is abundant, prâna
also appears in abundance, and where sunlight is absent,
prâna also is deficient.

Prâna emanates from the sun, and enters some of the
ultimate physical atoms which float about in the

H S I 66.   earth's atmosphere in countless myriads. Although we
say that this prânic force " enters " the physical atom,
it does not do so from outside : it enters from a higher

dimension, the fourth, and so appears to the clairvoyant as welling-up within the atom.

There are thus two forces which enter the atom from within : (1) the Will-force of the Logos, which holds the atom together in its proper shape ; (2) the Prânic force. It is important to note that Prâna comes from **F P 137.** the Second Aspect of the Solar Deity, whereas the Will-force emanates from the Third Aspect.

The effect of Prâna on atoms is entirely different

DIAGRAM II
THE VITALITY GLOBULE
(2) Vitality-Force enters Atom

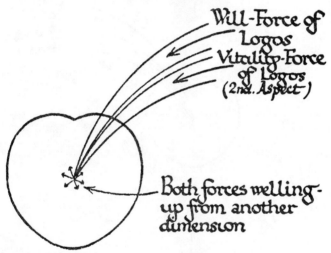

Will-Force of
Logos
Vitality-Force
of Logos
(2nd. Aspect)

Both forces welling-up from another dimension

from that of electricity, light, heat or other expressions of Fohat. Electricity, rushing through the atoms, deflects them and holds them in a certain way, and also **H S I 65.** imparts to them a separate and distinct vibration-rate. Any of the variants of Fohat, such as electricity, light or heat, cause an oscillation of the atom as a whole, an oscillation the size of which is enormous as compared with that of the atom itself, these forces of course acting on the atom from without.

Students of occultism will be familiar with the shape and structure of the ultimate physical atom, the smallest particle of matter on the physical plane, out of combinations of which are made the various combinations we know as solid, liquid, gas, etc. In the drawings in this book, therefore, these ultimate physical atoms are indicated as outlines only.

The force of Prâna, then, radiated from the sun, enters some of the atoms in the atmosphere and causes

DIAGRAM III
THE VITALITY GLOBULE
(3) The Atom Attracts 6 other Atoms

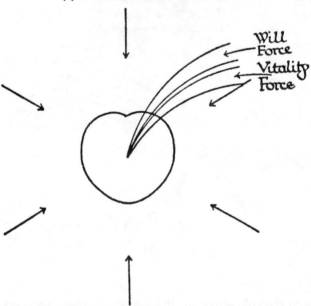

Will
Force
Vitality
Force

The Vitality Force " endows the atom with an additional life, and gives it a power of attraction. . . ."

H S I 66:
T B T 88. them to glow. Such an atom, charged with this additional life, has a six-fold power of attraction, so that it immediately draws round it six other atoms. These it arranges in a definite form, making what is termed in *Occult Chemistry* a hyper-meta-proto element, a combination of matter on the sub-atomic sub-plane. This combination, however, differs from all others so far observed, in that the force which creates it and holds

it together comes from the Second Aspect of the Solar H S I 67. Deity instead of from the Third. This form is known as the Vitality Globule, and is shown in the appended O C 45. drawing, which is enlarged from that on p. 45 of *Occult* H S I 67. *Chemistry.* This little group is the exceedingly brilliant

DIAGRAM II
THE VITALITY GLOBULE
(4) Formation of the Globule

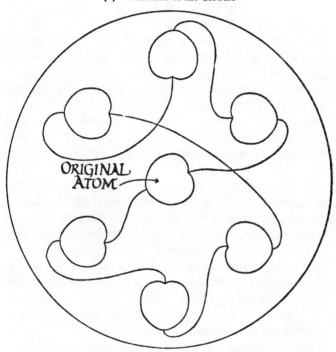

ORIGINAL ATOM

N.B.—The Vitality Globule is a hyper-meta-proto element, *i.e.*, on the sub-atomic level, and is unique in that it is created and held together by force emanating from the *Second Logos*. H.S.I., p. 67, O.C., p. 45.

bead upon the male or positive snake in the chemical element oxygen, and it is also the heart of the central globe in radium.

The globules, on account of their brilliance and extreme activity, can be seen by almost any one who cares to look, darting about in the atmosphere in immense numbers, especially on a sunny day. The H S I 67.

C W 64.

H S I 69.

H S I 68.

H S I 73-4.

H S I 84.

best way to see them is to face directly away from the sun and focus the eyes a few feet away, with a clear sky as background. Brilliant as is the globule, it is almost colourless, and may be compared to white light.

It has already been remarked that although the force which vivifies these globules is quite different from light, it nevertheless appears to depend upon light for its power of manifestation. In brilliant sunshine this vitality is constantly welling-up afresh, and the globules are generated in incredible numbers ; but in cloudy weather there is a great diminution in the number of globules formed, and during the night the operation appears to be entirely suspended. During the night, therefore, we may be said to be living upon the stock manufactured during the previous day, and although it appears practically impossible that it should ever be entirely exhausted, that stock evidently does run low when there is a long succession of cloudy days.

It is, of course, the work of the physical elemental to defend the body and to assimilate vitality (as will be described in detail in the next chapter) in order to recuperate the physical body. Whilst the physical body is awake, the nerves and muscles are kept tense, ready for instant action. When the body is asleep, the elemental lets the nerves and muscles relax and devotes himself especially to the assimilation of vitality. This accounts for the strong recuperative power of sleep, even of a momentary nap.

The elemental works most successfully during the early part of the night, when there is a copious supply of vitality. In the daily cycle the supply of globules is at its lowest ebb in the small hours of the morning, before sunrise, and this is one reason why so large a proportion of deaths occurs during those hours. Hence also the saying that an hour's sleep before midnight is worth two after it. Similarly, of course, the supply of prâna is at a lower ebb in winter than in summer.

Further, as Prâna is poured forth, not only on the physical, but also on all planes, emotion, intellect and

spirituality will be at their best under clear skies and
with the inestimable aid of sunlight. It may also be   *H S I* 85.
added that even the colours of etheric prâna correspond
to some extent to similar hues at the astral level.
Hence right feeling and clear thought react on the
physical and assist the latter to assimilate prâna and
thus maintain vigorous health. We thus find an
interesting light thrown on the intimate connection
between spiritual, mental and emotional health and
the health of the physical body, and are reminded of
the well-known saying of the Lord Buddha that the
first step on the road to Nirvâna is perfect physical
health.

The vitality globule, once charged, remains as a sub-   *H S I* 68.
atomic element, and does not appear to be subject to
any change or loss of force unless and until it is absorbed
by some living creature.

Before proceeding to study the extremely interesting
and important subject of the absorption of Prâna in the
physical body, we must first study the mechanism in
the Etheric Double by means of which this process is
effected.

* Since this book was compiled, *The Chakras*, by C. W. Leadbeater,
has appeared. In *The Chakras* it is stated that the three forces mentioned
are connected with the Outpourings, as follows :
The First Outpouring, from the Third Logos, is the Primary force
which manufactured the chemical elements.   This appears to be Fohat.
The Second Outpouring, from the Second Logos, has Prâna as *one* of
its aspects.
Kundalini is a further development, on the *ascending* arc, of the
First Outpouring.

CHAPTER III

FORCE-CENTRES

(See Diagrams III. (1), (2), (3), (4))

I L I **443.**   IN the Etheric Double, as well, incidentally, as in each of our other vehicles, there are certain Force-Centres, or Chakrams, as they are called in Sanskrit, this word meaning literally a wheel or revolving disc.

The chakrams are situated on the surface of the Double, that is about a quarter of an inch outside the skin of the body. To clairvoyant sight they appear as vortices or saucer-like depressions of rapidly rotating matter.

I L I **444.**   The forces flowing through the chakrams being essential to the life of the Etheric Double, every one

I L I **445.**   possesses such force-centres, though the degree of their development varies considerably in individuals. Where

I L I **447.**   they are undeveloped they glow dully and the etheric particles move sluggishly, just forming the vortex necessary for the transmission of the force, and no more : in developed people, on the other hand, the chakrams glow and pulsate, blazing with blinding brilliance like miniature suns. They vary in size from about two inches in diameter to about six inches.

S O S **257.**   In a new-born baby they are tiny little circles like a threepenny piece—little hard discs scarcely moving at all, and only faintly glowing.

I L I **451.**   The etheric chakrams have two distinct functions. The first is to absorb and distribute Prâna, or Vitality, to the etheric and thence to the physical body, thus keeping these alive. The second function is to bring down into the physical consciousness whatever may be the quality inherent in the corresponding astral centre. It is the lack of development of the etheric centres which accounts for the failure to bring into the physical brain memory of astral experiences. Many people are fully awake and vividly conscious on the astral plane and lead active lives in their astral bodies. When,

DIAGRAM III
STRUCTURE OF FORCE-CENTRE
(1) Shape

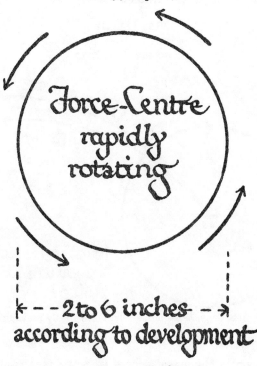

The appearance is that of a saucer-like depression, or vortex, in the surface of the Etheric Double, *i.e.*, ¼ inch outside the surface of the physical body.

Function : to convey forces from Astral to Etheric.

N.B.—Similar centres exist in all vehicles.

however, they return to their sleeping physical bodies, scarcely any memory of the astral life filters through into the brain, simply because the necessary etheric bridge is not built. When the etheric centres are fully developed, there is full and continuous memory of astral experiences in the brain.

I L I 450.   There appears to be no connection between the activity or development of the etheric chakrams and moral qualities: the two developments are quite distinct.

I L I 451.   Although there is in the astral body an astral centre corresponding to each of the etheric centres, yet as the astral centre is a vortex in four dimensions, it extends in a direction quite different from the etheric, and

DIAGRAM III

STRUCTURE OF FORCE-CENTRE

(2) Inrush of Vital Force

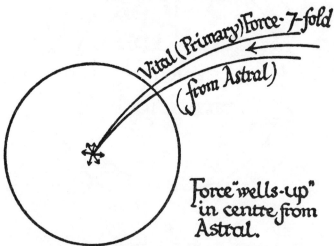

One of the seven varieties of the Vital Force greatly predominates in each centre.

This inrush of Vital Force brings life to the physical body.

consequently the astral centre is by no means always coterminous with the corresponding etheric centre, though some part of it is always coincident. Whilst the etheric centres are always on the surface of the etheric body, the astral centre is frequently in the interior of the astral body.

I L I 444.   We have already seen (Chapter II.) that there are seven varieties of Prâna, all of which are present in all the chakrams; but in each chakram one of the varieties is always greatly predominant.

The Prâna rushes into the centre of each chakram, *I L I* 444.
from a direction at right angles to the plane of the
chakram ; " welling-up " would perhaps be a better
term, as the force comes from the astral plane into the
etheric. From the centre of the chakram the force
then radiates at right angles to the direction from *I L I* 445-6.
which it came, *i.e.*, in the plane of the surface of the
Etheric Double, in a number of directions, and in
straight lines. The number of directions, which are

DIAGRAM III
STRUCTURE OF FORCE-CENTRE
(3) Formation of " Spokes "

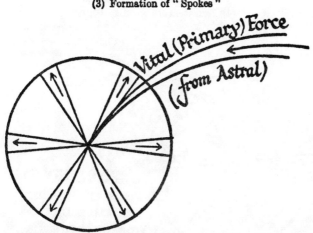

The Primary Force " wells-up " at centre, and then rushes outwards
radially along " spokes," the number of these " spokes " differing in each
centre.

similar to the spokes of a wheel, is different in each
chakram.

The spokes divide the chakram into a number of
segments, like the petals of a flower : hence, in Hindu
books, the chakrams are often described as resembling
flowers.

Now somewhat as a bar-magnet thrust into a coil of
wire will set up or " induce " a current of electricity in
the wire at right angles to the axis of the magnet, so
does the primary force of Prâna entering the chakram

set up or induce secondary forces in the plane of the chakram. These secondary forces spin round the chakram, passing over and under the spokes, much as the material of the bottom of a circular basket passes over and under the ribs which radiate from the centre.

Each of these secondary forces, sweeping round the chakram, has its own characteristic wave-length, and in addition moves, not in straight lines, but in relatively large undulations, each of which is a multiple of the

DIAGRAM III

STRUCTURE OF FORCE-CENTRE

(4) Formation of Secondary Forces

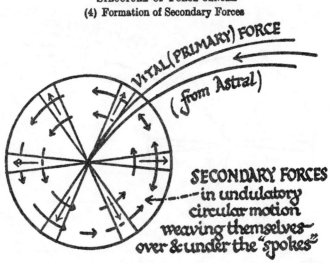

VITAL (PRIMARY) FORCE

(from Astral)

SECONDARY FORCES
in undulatory
circular motion
weaving themselves
over & under the "spokes"

wave-length within it. The wave-lengths are very minute, and probably some thousands of them are included in one undulation, though the exact proportion has not yet been determined. The general effect is shimmering and iridescent, like mother-of-pearl, or a certain variety of Venetian glass.

I L I 443.   The chakrams are often spoken of as corresponding to certain physical organs, those organs, in fact, which are the nearest to them ; but, as already mentioned, the chakrams themselves are not in the interior of the body, but on the surface of the Etheric Double.

The list of the chakrams and their names is as
follows :—

NO.	NEAREST PHYSICAL ORGAN.	SANSKRIT NAME.
1 2 3 4 5 6 7	Base of Spine. Navel. Spleen. Heart. Throat. Between Eyebrows. Top of Head.	Mûladhâra. Manipûra. Svâdhisthâna. Anâhata. Visuddha. Ajnâ. Sahasrâra Brahmarandhra.
8 9 10	Lower Organs.	

Numbers 8, 9 and 10, connected with the lower
organs of the body, are not used by students of the
" white " magic, though there are certain schools in   *I L I* 444.
existence which make use of them. The dangers connected with them are so serious that we should consider
their awakening as the greatest of misfortunes.

The flow of vitality into or through any chakram is   *H S I* 80.
quite separate and distinct from the development of the
chakram brought about by the awakening of Kundalini,
which will be described in Chapter XIII.

We shall now proceed to study each of the seven
chakrams in turn, examining its structure, appearance,
function, and the faculties associated with it.   For
reasons which will presently appear, it will be convenient to commence with the third centre, that situated
near the spleen.

CHAPTER IV

THE SPLEEN CENTRE

(See Diagrams IV (1), (2), (3), (4))

H S I 69;
I L I 448.

THE spleen centre has six spokes, and therefore the same number of petals or undulations. In appearance it is specially radiant, glowing and sun-like.

This centre is unique in this, that it has the all-

DIAGRAM IV
SPLEEN CENTRE
(1) Structure

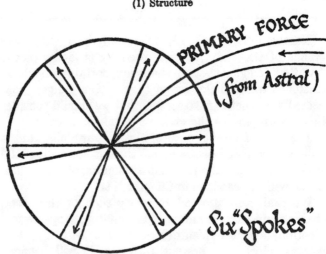

General appearance " Radiant and sun-like."
Function of Astral Centre: vitalises Astral Body. Power to travel consciously.
Function of Etheric Centre: vitalises Physical Body, Memory of Astral journeys.

M V 129;
I L I 448.

important function of absorbing the Vitality Globules from the atmosphere, disintegrating them, and distributing the component atoms charged with the

DIAGRAM IV
SPLEEN CENTRE
(2) Absorption of Vitality Globules

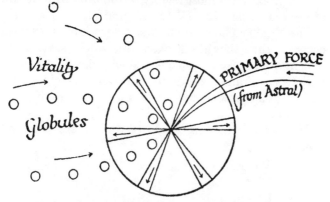

Vitality Globules are drawn into centre of Force-Centre.

DIAGRAM IV
SPLEEN CENTRE
(3) Decomposition of Vitality Globules

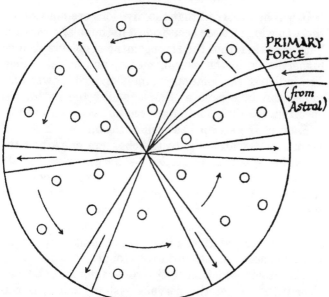

Vitality globules, after being drawn into Centre, are decomposed, and
the component particles are whirled round by the "Secondary Forces."

specialised and transmuted Prâna, to the various parts
of the body.

The process will most readily be followed with the aid
of the diagrams, Nos. IV (2), (3) and (4).

H S I 69.

The Vitality Globules are first drawn into the spleen
centre : then they are broken up into the seven component atoms, each atom charged with one of the seven
varieties of Prâna : these atoms are then caught up by
the rotating secondary forces and spun round the
chakram.

The seven different kinds of Prâna are coloured
thus :—

> Violet.
> Blue.
> Green.
> Yellow.
> Orange.
> Dark Red.
> Rose-Red.

H S I 70.

It will be observed that the divisions are not exactly
those to which we are accustomed in the solar spectrum,
but resemble rather the arrangement of colours seen on
higher levels in the causal, mental and astral bodies.
The indigo of the solar spectrum is divided between the
violet and blue rays of Prâna, whilst the red of the
spectrum is split up into dark red and rose-red Prâna.

H S I 70.

Each of the six spokes then seizes on one variety of
atom and despatches it to the chakram or part of the
body for which it is needed.   This accounts for six
kinds of atoms only : the seventh variety, that coloured
rose-pink, is despatched through the hub or centre of
the spleen chakram itself, whence it is distributed over
the whole of the nervous system.   These rose-coloured
atoms are the original atoms which first drew round
them the six others to form the globule.

H S I 72.

The atoms which bear the rose-coloured Prâna are
clearly the life of the nervous system, and it is this
variety of Prâna which one man may give to another,
as described in Chapter XIII.   If the nerves are insuf-

ficiently supplied with this rose-coloured Prâna, they become sensitive and intensely irritable; the patient finds himself restless, and the least noise or touch is agony to him. Instant relief may be afforded him by

DIAGRAM IV

SPLEEN CENTRE

(4) Dispersion of Vitality Particles

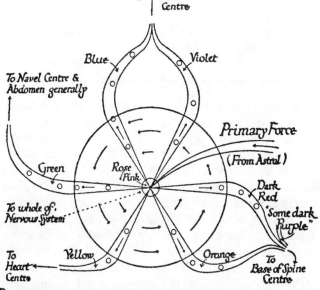

Process :—

1. Vitality globules are drawn into Centre.
2. Vitality globules are broken up into particles.
3. Vitality particles are whirled round by " secondary " forces.
4. Vitality particles are seized by appropriate " spoke," and despatched to destination shown.

N.B.—The rose-pink atoms are the original atoms which first drew round them 6 others to form the globule.

some healthy person flooding his nervous system with a supply of rose-coloured Prâna.

Although there are seven distinct kinds of Prâna, there are only five main streams, as described in some Indian books, because after issuing from the spleen chakram the blue and the violet join into one stream and the orange and dark red join into another stream. The streams leave the spleen centre horizontally.

H S I 71.

I L I 448.

D

The colours of the streams and their destinations are as set out in the following table :—

NO.	STREAM.	DESTINATION.
1	Violet-Blue.	Throat Centre.
2	Green.	Navel Centre and Abdomen generally.
3	Yellow.	Heart Centre.
4	Orange-Dark Red (and some Dark Purple).	Base of Spine Centre.
5	Rose-Red.	Nervous System.

H S I 70-72.

As the various kinds of Prâna-charged atoms are distributed where required, the charge of Prâna is withdrawn from them, precisely as a charge of electricity might be withdrawn. The Prâna gives life to the Etheric Double and, through that, to the dense body, the degree of health of the parts of the body being largely determined by the volume of Prâna distributed. The bearing of this significant fact on the maintenance of physical vigour and the cure of disease is clearly of very great importance and will be more fully considered in the section devoted to Healing and Mesmerism.

H S I 77.

The atoms bearing the rose-coloured Prâna grow gradually paler as they sweep along the nerves and part with their Prânic content. They are eventually discharged from the body through the pores of the skin (as well as in other ways), forming what is called the health aura, a pale bluish-white emanation, of which a plate is given in *Man, Visible and Invisible*, page 128.

H S I 79.

In a man in vigorous health the spleen does its work so generously that considerably more of the particles charged with Prâna are present than the man requires for his own use. These unused particles are discharged from the body in all directions, through the health aura, along with the particles from which the Prâna has been extracted. Such a man is thus a source of health and strength to those around him, constantly though uncon-

M V 128.
M V 130.

M V 130;
H S I 72.

sciously shedding vitality on any who may be in his
vicinity. This process may be considerably intensified
by those who definitely set themselves to heal others,
by mesmeric passes and otherwise, as we shall see more
fully in a later chapter.

In addition to these particles just mentioned, it is   *M V* 131.
also well known that small particles of dense physical
matter are continually being thrown off from a man's
body, in insensible perspiration and in other ways. A
clairvoyant sees these particles as a faint grey mist.
Many of the particles are crystalline in form and therefore appear as geometrical figures; one of the commonest
is that of common salt, or sodium chloride, which takes
the form of cubes.

A man, on the other hand, who is unable for any   *M V* 131.
reason to specialise for his own use a sufficient amount
of Prâna, frequently and also unconsciously acts as a
sponge, his physical elemental drawing vitality from   *H S I* 74.
any sensitive person who happens to be near, to his
own temporary benefit, but often to the serious injury
of the victim. This phenomenon largely accounts for
those feelings of weariness and languor which come over
one after being near people who, not being very strong
themselves, possess this unfortunate vampire-like
faculty of draining others of vitality. The same thing
may happen, often in an aggravated form, at spiritualistic séances.

The vegetable kingdom also absorbs vitality, but   *H S I* 75.
seems in most cases to use only a small part of it. Many
trees, especially the pine and eucalyptus, extract from
the globules almost exactly the same constituents as
does the higher part of man's etheric body, and reject
any superfluous atoms charged with rose-coloured
Prâna which they do not themselves require. Hence
the proximity of such trees is extremely beneficial for
people who are nervously depleted.

The health aura, consisting of these particles ejected
from the body, serves the useful purpose of protecting
the man from the invasion of disease germs. In health
the particles are thrown out through the pores in

M V 132. straight lines, at right angles to the surface of the body, giving to the health aura a striated effect. As long as the lines remain firm and straight the body seems to be almost entirely protected from the attack of evil physical influences, such as disease germs, the germs M V 133. being actually repelled and carried away by the out-rush of Prânic force. But when, on account of weakness, over-fatigue, a wound, depression of spirits, or through the excesses of an irregular life, an unusually large amount of Prâna is required to repair waste or damage within the body, and there is consequently a serious diminution in the quantity radiated, the lines of the health aura droop, become erratic and confused, the system of defence is weakened, and it is then compara-tively easy for deadly germs to effect an entrance (*vide M., V. & I.*, p. 132, Plate XXV.).

N F F 220. In the *Science of Breath*, translated by Râma Prasâd, it is stated that the natural length from the body to the periphery of the " halo " of Prâna, is 10 " fingers " during inspiration of the breath and 12 during ex-piration. At other times the lengths are stated to be as follows : in eating and speaking, 18 ; in walking, 24 ; in running, 42 ; in cohabitation, 65 ; in sleeping, 100. A reduction in length is said to result when a man over-comes desire, gains the 8 Siddhis, etc. It seems probable, though by no means certain, that the " halo " mentioned is the health aura. The term " fingers " here means, in accordance with the method of reckon-ing used in India, not the length of a finger but its width.

Both etheric matter and Prâna are very readily amenable to the human will. It is possible, therefore, to protect oneself to a considerable extent from the M V 133. hostile influences mentioned above, by making an effort of the will to check the radiation of vitality at the outer extremity of the health aura, building it there into a wall or shell which will be impervious to disease germs and also prevent the vitality from being sucked away by any one near who has the vampire tendency.

With a little further effort a shell may be made impervious also to astral or mental influence.

The question of etheric shells is so important that it will be necessary later on in this book to enter into it rather more fully than we have done here, where we are dealing purely with the health aura.

The development of the spleen centre enables the *I L I* 457. man to remember his astral journeys, though sometimes only very partially, the faculty associated with the corresponding astral centre being that of travelling *I L I* 453. consciously in the astral body. Those vague memories, *I L I* 457. that most of us have, of blissful flights through the air are often due to slight or accidental stimulation of the spleen chakram.

It may be mentioned, in passing, that the astral *I L I* 453. centre corresponding to the spleen also has the function of vitalising the whole astral body.

CHAPTER V

THE BASE OF THE SPINE CENTRE

(See Diagrams V. (*a*) and (*b*))

I L I 447–8.　THE first centre, or chakram, at the base of the spine, has a primary force which radiates in four spokes, making the centre appear to be divided into quadrants, with hollows between them, like a cross, a symbol which is often used to represent this centre.

When aroused into full activity, this centre is fiery

DIAGRAM V
BASE OF SPINE CENTRE
(*a*) Normal Person

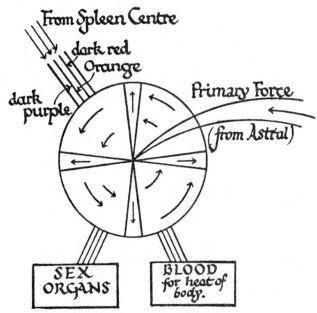

Function of Astral Centre: Seat of Kundalini.
Function of Etheric Centre: Seat of Kundalini.
Appearance: " Fiery orange-red." Number of " spokes," four.
N.B.—Kundalini has seven layers or degrees of force.

DIAGRAM V
BASE OF SPINE CENTRE
(b) Developed Person

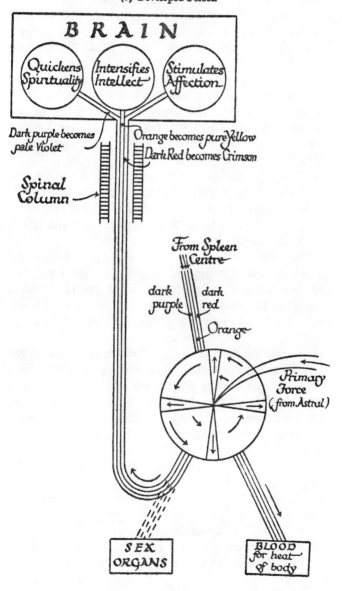

BRAIN

Quickens Spirituality

Intensifies Intellect

Stimulates Affection

Dark purple becomes pale Violet

Orange becomes pure Yellow
Dark Red becomes Crimson

Spinal Column

From Spleen Centre

dark purple   dark red

Orange

Primary Force (from Astral)

SEX ORGANS

BLOOD for heat of body

orange-red in colour, corresponding closely with the stream of dark red and orange vitality which comes to it from the spleen centre. It may be mentioned that in every case there is a similar correspondence between the colour of the stream of vitality flowing into a centre and the colour of the centre itself.

In addition to the orange and darker reds, there is also some dark purple vitality flowing into this centre, rather as though the spectrum bent round in a circle and the colours began again at a lower octave.

H S I 76.

From this centre the orange-red ray flows to the generative organs, energising the sexual nature : it also seems to enter the blood and keep up the heat of the body.

A very remarkable and important effect can be produced by a person who persistently refuses to yield to the lower nature. By long and determined effort the orange-red ray can be deflected upwards to the brain, where all three of its constituents undergo a profound modification. The orange is raised into pure yellow and intensifies the intellectual powers. The dark red becomes crimson and increases the power of unselfish affection ; the dark purple is transmuted into a beautiful pale violet, quickening the spiritual part of the nature.

The seat of Kundalini, the Serpent-Fire, is in the base of the spine centre. This will be dealt with in a later chapter : for the present we may just note that a man who has achieved the transmutation just mentioned will find that sensual desires no longer trouble him, and when it becomes necessary for him to arouse the serpent-fire he will be free from the most serious of the dangers of that process. When a man has finally completed the change, the orange-red ray passes straight into the centre at the base of the spine, and thence runs upwards through the hollow of the vertebral column and so to the brain.

H S I 77.

I L I 447.

A flaming cross is a symbol sometimes used to represent the serpent-fire residing in the base of the spine centre.

CHAPTER VI

THE NAVEL CENTRE

(See Diagram VI)

THE second centre, at the navel or solar plexus, *I L I* 448. receives a primary force which radiates in ten directions, there being ten undulations or petals.

Its predominant colour is a curious blending of various shades of red, though there is also a great deal of green in it. It receives the green ray from the *H S I* 72. spleen centre, that ray also flooding the abdomen, vivifying the liver, kidneys, intestines, and the digestive

DIAGRAM VI
NAVEL CENTRE

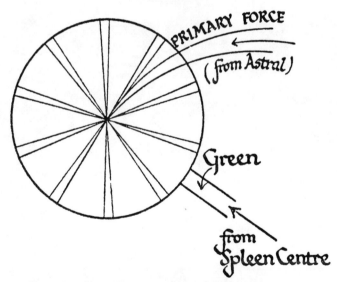

Function of Astral Centre : Feeling : general sensitiveness.
Function of Etheric Centre : Feeling astral influences.
Appearance : " various shades of red, with much green." Number of " spokes," ten.

apparatus generally, centering especially in the solar
plexus.

I L I 448.   The centre is closely associated with feelings and
emotions of various kinds. The corresponding astral
centre, when awakened, gives the power of feeling, a
sensitiveness to all sorts of influences, though without
I L 452-3.   as yet anything like the definite comprehension that
comes from the faculties corresponding to seeing or
I L I 457.   hearing. When, therefore, the etheric centre becomes
active, the man begins in the physical body to be
conscious of astral influences, vaguely feeling friendli-
ness and hostility, or that some places are pleasant and
others unpleasant, but without in the least knowing why.

The Sanskrit name for this centre is Manipûra.

CHAPTER VII

THE HEART CENTRE

(See Diagram VII)

HAVING already dealt with the third centre, that near the spleen, we pass next to the fourth centre, that of the heart.

This chakram has twelve spokes or radiations, and is a glowing golden colour. It receives the yellow ray from the spleen centre; when the current is full and

I L I 448.
H S I 71.
H S I 77.

DIAGRAM VII
HEART CENTRE

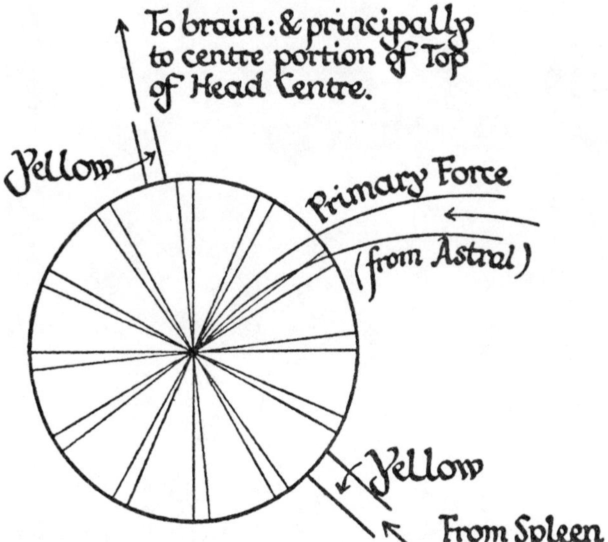

N.B.—The Yellow Ray permeates the blood, and is carried all over the body with it.

Function of Astral Centre : Comprehension of Astral vibrations.
Function of Etheric Centre : Consciousness of feelings of others.
Appearance : " glowing golden." Number of " spokes," 12.

strong it produces strength and regularity in the heart action. Flowing round the heart chakram, the yellow ray also interpenetrates the blood and thus is carried all over the body. It also passes on to the brain and permeates it, though directing itself principally to the twelve-petalled flower in the middle of the seventh or highest centre. In the brain it confers the power of high philosophical and metaphysical thought.

I L I 453.

The corresponding astral centre, when awakened, endows a man with the power to comprehend and sympathise with, and so instinctively understand, the feelings of other astral entities.

I L I 458.

The etheric centre, therefore, makes a man aware, in his physical consciousness, of the joys and sorrows of others, and sometimes even causes him to reproduce in himself by sympathy their physical aches and pains.

The Sanskrit for this chakram is Anâhata.

CHAPTER VIII

THE THROAT CENTRE

(See Diagram VIII)

THIS chakram, the fifth, has sixteen spokes, and, *I L I* 449. therefore, sixteen petals or divisions. In colour it shows a good deal of blue. but its general effect is silvery and gleaming, not unlike moonlight on rippling water.

It receives the violet-blue ray from the spleen

DIAGRAM VIII
THROAT CENTRE

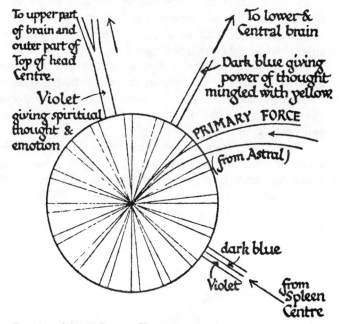

To upper part of brain and outer part of Top of head Centre.

To lower & Central brain

Dark blue giving power of thought mingled with yellow.

Violet giving spiritual thought & emotion

PRIMARY FORCE

(from Astral)

dark blue

Violet

from Spleen Centre

Function of Astral Centre : Hearing.
Function of Etheric Centre : Etheric and Astral hearing.
Appearance : " Silvery and gleaming, with a good deal of blue."
Number of " spokes," 16.

H S I 71.

chakram. This ray then appears to divide, the light blue remaining to course through and vivify the throat-centre, while the dark blue and violet pass on to the brain.

II S I 78.

The light blue gives health to the region of the throat, the strength and elasticity of the vocal chords of a great singer or speaker, for example, being accompanied by special brilliance and activity of this ray.

II S I 71.

The dark blue expends itself in the lower central parts of the brain, while the violet floods the upper part and appears to give special vigour to the chakram at the top of the head, diffusing itself chiefly through the nine hundred and sixty petals of the outer part of that centre.

H S I 78.

Ordinary thought is stimulated by the blue ray, mingled with part of the yellow (from the heart centre, *vide* Chapter VII.).

In some forms of idiocy the yellow and blue-violet flow to the brain is almost entirely inhibited.

Thought and emotion of a high spiritual type seem to depend largely upon the violet ray.

I L I 453.

The awakening of the corresponding astral centre gives the power of hearing on the astral plane, that is to say, the faculty which produces in the astral world the effect similar to that which in the physical world we call hearing.

I L I 458.

When the etheric centre is aroused, the man in his physical consciousness hears voices, which sometimes make all kinds of suggestions to him. He may hear music, or other less pleasant sounds. When fully working, it makes a man clairaudient so far as the etheric and astral planes are concerned.

The Sanskrit name for this centre is Visuddha.

CHAPTER IX

THE CENTRE BETWEEN THE EYEBROWS

(See Diagram IX)

THE sixth centre, that between the eyebrows, has *I L I* 449. ninety-six spokes. In Indian books, however, it is mentioned as having only two petals, this being probably due to the fact that it presents the appearance of being divided into halves. Of these, the one is predominantly rose-coloured, though with a great deal

DIAGRAM IX
BETWEEN-THE-EYEBROWS CENTRE

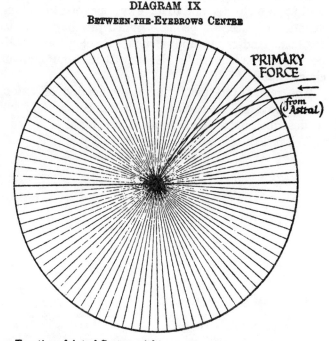

Function of Astral Centre: sight.
Function of Etheric Centre: Clairvoyance: Magnification.
Appearance: half " predominantly rose, with much yellow "; **half** " predominantly a kind of purplish blue." Number of " spokes," 96.

THE ETHERIC DOUBLE

of yellow in it, and the other predominantly a kind of purplish-blue.

The writer has been unable to find any specific description of the source of the Prânic stream which flows into this centre, though it is mentioned in *The Inner Life*, page 449, that the purplish-blue appearance of one half of the centre agrees closely with the colours of the special types of vitality that vivify it. This would seem to indicate the dark blue (and violet ?) ray which passes the throat centre and proceeds to the brain.

I L I 453. The development of the corresponding astral centre confers the power to perceive definitely the nature and shape of astral objects, instead of vaguely sensing their presence.

I L I 458. The awakening of the etheric centre causes a man to begin to see objects, and to have various sorts of waking visions of places or people. When just beginning to awaken, landscapes and clouds of colour are half-perceived. When fully developed it brings about clairvoyance.

The remarkable faculty of magnification of vision, or its converse, is associated with this centre, and will be described in the chapter on Etheric Sight.

In Sanskrit this centre is known as A'jnā.

CHAPTER X

THE CENTRE AT THE TOP OF THE HEAD

(See Diagram X)

THIS centre, the seventh, situated at the top of the head, is somewhat different in construction from the other six. It is described in Indian books as the thousand-petalled lotus, though the actual number of radiations of the primary force is 960. In addition to this, it possesses a sort of subsidiary whirlpool or minor activity in its central portion, which has twelve undulations of its own. *I L I* 449. *I L I* 450.

When fully alive, this chakram is perhaps the most resplendent of all, full of indescribable chromatic effects and vibrating with almost inconceivable rapidity. The central portion is gleaming white, flushed with gold in its heart.

This centre receives in its outer portion the violet ray which passes through the throat centre, while in its central portion it receives the yellow ray from the heart centre.

The arousing of the corresponding astral centre rounds off and completes the astral life, endowing a man with the perfection of his faculties. *I L I* 454.

With one type of individual, the astral chakrams corresponding to the sixth and seventh etheric chakrams both converge upon the pituitary body, the latter organ being practically the only direct link between the physical and higher planes.

With another type of person, however, while the sixth chakram is still attached to the pituitary body, the seventh is bent or slanted until it coincides with the atrophied organ known as the pineal gland, which with people of this type becomes a line of direct

E

communication with the lower mental, without apparently passing through the intermediate astral plane in

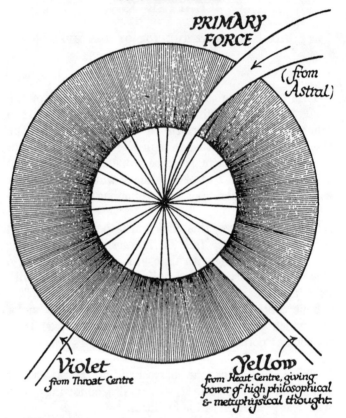

DIAGRAM X
Top-of-Head Centre

PRIMARY
FORCE
(from Astral)

Violet
from Throat Centre

Yellow
from Heart Centre, giving
power of high philosophical
& metaphysical thought.

Appearance :
    Central portion : " gleaming white, flushed with gold."
    Outer portion : "most resplendent of all, full of indescribable
       chromatic effects."
Number of " spokes " : Central portion 12, outer portion 960.
Function of Astral Centre : perfects and completes faculties.
Function of Etheric Centre : gives continuity of consciousness.

the ordinary way. This explains the emphasis sometimes laid on the development of the pineal gland.

The awakening of the etheric centre enables a man
through it to leave the physical body in full conscious-

ness, and also to re-enter it without the usual break, so that his consciousness will be continuous through night and day.

The real reason for tonsure, as practised by the Roman Church, was to leave uncovered the brahmarandra chakram, so that there might be not even the slightest hindrance in the way of psychic force which in their meditations the candidates were intended to try to arouse. *S O S* 289.

CHAPTER XI

DISCHARGES

(See Diagram XI)

JUST as the dense physical body uses up its materials, and discharges its waste products through the five excretory organs—the skin, lungs, liver, intestines and kidneys—so does the etheric body use up the material with which it is supplied, through physical food and the absorption of the Vitality Globule, and discharge its waste particles in various ways.

A Chart of these discharges is appended, the results it shows being described as follows.

H S I 79. Through the breath and the pores of the skin are expelled both the bluish-white particles from which the Prâna has been extracted, such particles still charged with rose-coloured Prâna as are superfluous to the requirements of the body, and also the atoms from the blue rays used by the throat centre.

Through the lower excretory organs pass the emptied atoms of the green ray, from the digestive system, and also, in the case of the ordinary man, those of the red-orange ray.

Through the top of the head pass the atoms from the dark blue and violet rays.

In a developed person, however, who has achieved the deflection upwards of the red-orange ray, the particles from this ray are discharged through the top
H S I 80. of the head. These form a fiery cascade, frequently shown as a flame in ancient statues of the Buddha and other saints.

Atoms which have been emptied of Prâna become once more precisely like any other atoms. Some of them are absorbed by the body and enter into the various combinations which are constantly being made, while others which are not required are thrown off through any convenient channel.

In addition to the above, the matter of the Etheric *H S I* 82.

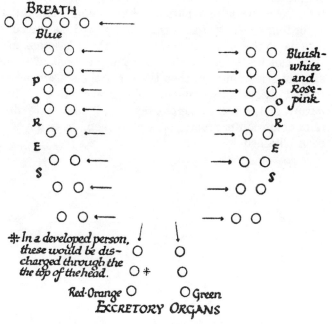

DIAGRAM XI
DISCHARGES

N.B.—Some of the particles, when depleted of vitality, are used up for building or nourishing the Etheric Body.

Double itself is also constantly being thrown out of the body through the pores of the skin, just as is gaseous matter. Consequently persons who are near one another are liable to absorb each other's etheric emanations.

H S I I 25.   The radiation of etheric matter is strongest from the ends of the fingers and toes : hence the great importance of scrupulous cleanliness in these parts of the body : a person with dirt under the finger nails, for example, is continually pouring forth a stream of unhealthy influence into the etheric world.

I L I I 192-3.   The physical emanations of the body, consisting largely of finely-divided salts, appear to clairvoyant sight as multitudes of tiny forms, such as dice, stars, and double pyramids. The character of these tiny particles may be affected by loss of health, by a wave of emotion, or even a definite train of thought. In this connection Professor Gates is reported as saying (*a*) that the material emanations of the living body differ according to the states of the mind as well as the conditions of the physical health ; (*b*) that these emanations can be tested by the chemical reactions of some salts of selenium ; (*c*) that these reactions are characterised by various tints or colours according to the nature of the mental impressions : (*d*) that forty different emotion-products, as he calls them, have already been obtained.

CHAPTER XII

TABULATION OF RESULTS

(See Diagrams XII., XIII., and Chart)

FOR the convenience and ready reference of the student, a summary of the processes described in

DIAGRAM XII
DISTRIBUTION CHART

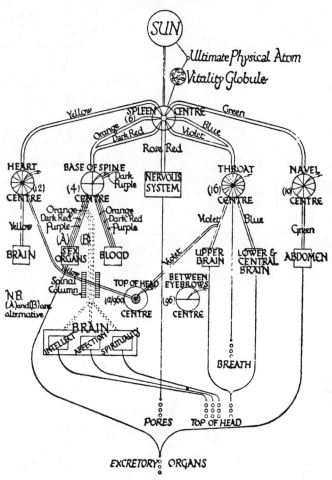

NO.	PLACE.	SPOKES.	APPEARANCE.	VITALITY RECEIVED.	VITALITY SENT OUT.
1	Base of Spine.	4	Fiery orange-red.	Orange and red, from Spleen Centre : also some dark purple.	..
2	Navel.	10	Various shades of red, with much green.	Green, from Spleen Centre.	..
3	Spleen.	6	Radiant and sun-like.	..	(1) Violet-blue, to Throat. (2) Yellow, to Heart. (3) Green, to Solar Plexus. (4) Rose, to Nervous System (5) Orange-red, to Base o. Spine, with some darl purple.
4	Heart.	12	Glowing golden.	Yellow, from Spleen Centre.	Yellow, to Blood, Brain an middle of Top of Hea Centre.
5	Throat.	16	Silvery and gleaming with much blue.	Violet - blue, from Spleen Centre.	Dark blue, to Lower and Central Brain. Violet, t Upper Brain and oute part of Top of Hea Centre.
6	Between Eyebrows.	96	Half : Rose, with much yellow. Half : Purplish-blue.	?	..
7	Top of Head.	12	Centre : gleaming white and gold.	Yellow, from Heart Centre.	..
		960	Outer part : full of indescribable chromatic effects.	Violet, from Throat Centre.	..
8 9 10	} Not used in " white magic."			..	..
1	*In Developed Person.* Base of Spine.	4	Fiery orange-red.	Orange and red, from Spleen Centre, and some dark purple.	..

OF CENTRES, ETC.

NO.	REGION VITALISED.	FUNCTION OF ASTRAL CENTRE.	FUNCTION OF ETHERIC CENTRE.
1	Sex organs. Blood, for heat of body.	Seat of Kundalini. Kundalini goes to each Centre in turn and vivifies it.	Seat of Kundalini. Kundalini goes to each Centre in turn and vivifies it.
2	Solar plexus, Liver, Kidneys, Intestines and Abdomen generally.	Feeling : general sensitiveness.	Feeling astral influences.
3	..	Vitalises Astral Body. Power to travel consciously.	Vitalises Physical Body. Memory of astral journeys.
4	Heart.	Comprehension of Astral Vibrations.	Consciousness of feelings of others.
5	..	Hearing.	Etheric and Astral hearing.
6	..	Sight.	Clairvoyance. Magnification.
7	..	Perfects and completes faculties.	Continuity of consciousness.
8 9 10	..	..	..
1	Orange, through Spinal Column, to Brain : becomes yellow and stimulates intellect. Dark red, through Spinal Column, to Brain : becomes crimson and stimulates affection. Dark purple, through Spinal Column, to Brain : becomes pale violet and stimulates spirituality.		..

DIAGRAM XIII
MAN AND HIS ETHERIC CENTRES

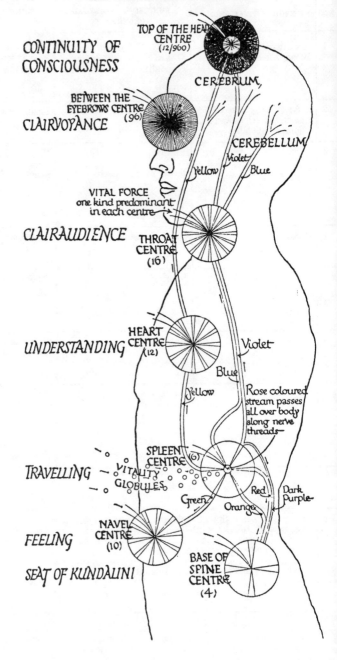

CONTINUITY OF CONSCIOUSNESS

TOP OF THE HEAD CENTRE (12/960)

CEREBRUM

BETWEEN THE EYEBROWS CENTRE (96)

CLAIRVOYANCE

CEREBELLUM

Yellow   Violet   Blue

VITAL FORCE one kind predominant in each centre

CLAIRAUDIENCE   THROAT CENTRE (16)

UNDERSTANDING   HEART CENTRE (12)

Violet

Blue

Yellow

Rose coloured stream passes all over body along nerve threads

SPLEEN CENTRE (6)

TRAVELLING   VITALITY GLOBULES

Green   Orange   Red   Dark Purple

NAVEL CENTRE (10)

FEELING

BASE OF SPINE CENTRE (4)

SEAT OF KUNDALINI

Chapters II. to XI. is given in the tabular statement appended.

The same information is also given in the form of a Distribution Chart, which gives a synthesis of these processes in graphic form, from the emanation of Prâna from the sun to the discharge from the body of the particles from which the Prâna has been extracted.

In a still further diagram is shown an outline of the human body with the approximate position of the etheric centres, the streams of vitality and other useful information.

CHAPTER XIII

KUNDALINI

I L I 461-2. As we have already seen, Kundalini, or the Serpent-Fire, is one of the forces which emanate from the sun, and is entirely separate and distinct from both Fohat and Prâna, being, so far as is known, incapable of being converted into any form of these other forces.

Kundalini has been variously called the Serpent-Fire, the Fiery Power, and the World's Mother. To clairvoyant vision it appears in very truth like liquid fire as it rushes through the body, and the course through which it ought to move is a spiral one like the coils of a serpent. The name of World's Mother is appropriate because through it our various vehicles may be vivified.

I L I 130. An ancient symbol of the spinal column and Kundalini is that of the thyrsus, which is a staff with a pine cone on its top. In India the same symbol is found, but instead of the staff a stick of bamboo with seven knots is used, the knots of course representing the seven chakrams or force centres. In some modifications of the mysteries a hollow iron rod, said to contain fire, was used instead of the thyrsus. It is said that the modern barber's pole, which is certainly a very ancient symbol, with its spiral bands and a knob on the end, has a similar significance, the modern barber being descended from the ancient chirurgeons or surgeons, who also practised alchemy, a science originally spiritual rather than material.

Kundalini exists on all planes of which we know anything, and it also appears to have seven layers or degrees of force.

I L I 452-3. The astral body originally was an almost inert mass, with only the vaguest consciousness, with no definite power of doing anything, and no clear knowledge of the world which surrounds it.   Kundalini was then awakened at the astral level, in the centre corresponding to the base of the spine centre.   It moved to the second centre, near the navel, and vivified it, thereby awakening in the astral body the power of feeling, of sensitiveness without definite comprehension.

Kundalini then passed to the third (spleen), fourth (heart), fifth (throat), sixth (eyebrows) and seventh (top of head) centre in turn, awakening in each the various powers already described in previous chapters.

The mechanism by means of which we become aware of astral happenings is interesting and should be clearly grasped by the student.   Although in the physical body we have special organs, each located in a definite and fixed part of the body, for seeing, hearing, and the rest, an entirely different arrangement is made in the astral body, specialised organs not being necessary for the attainment of the result aimed at. *I L I* 455.

The matter of the astral body is in a condition of constant movement, the particles flowing and swirling about like those of boiling water, and all of them pass in turn through each of the force-centres.   Each of these centres then has the power of evoking from the particles of the astral body the ability to respond to a certain set of vibrations, corresponding to what in the physical world we call vibrations of light, sound, heat, and so forth.   When, therefore, the astral centres are vivified and in working order, they confer these various powers on the whole of the matter of the astral body, so that the latter is enabled to exercise its powers in every part of itself.   Consequently a man functioning in his astral body can see equally well objects in front of him, behind, above or below.   The chakramś or centres, therefore, cannot be described as organs of sense in the ordinary sense of that term, though they do convey the powers of sense to the astral body. *I L I* 456.

I L I 455.

But even when these astral senses are fully awake, it by no means follows that the man will be able to bring through into his physical body any consciousness *I L I* 456.

of their action. He may, in fact, in his physical consciousness know nothing whatever of it. The only way in which the consciousness of these astral experiences can be brought into the physical brain is by means of the corresponding etheric centres, which must first be awakened and made active.

The method of awakening is precisely similar to that adopted in the astral body, *i.e.*, by arousing Kundalini, which lies dormant in etheric matter in the centre near the base of the spine.

I L I 457.

The arousing is achieved by a determined and long-continued effort of the will, bringing the centre at the base of the spine into activity being, in fact, precisely the awakening of Kundalini. When once this is aroused, it is by its tremendous force that the other centres are vivified in turn. The effect on the centres is to bring into the physical consciousness the powers which were aroused by the development of the corresponding astral centres.

In order to bring about these results, however, it is necessary that the serpent-fire move to the chakrams in a certain order, and in a certain way, which varies

I L I 477.
I L I 465.

with different types of people. Occultists who understand these matters from first-hand knowledge are always exceedingly careful to give no clue to the order in which the serpent-fire should be passed through the centres. The reason for this is on account of the very serious dangers, the gravity of which can scarcely be exaggerated, awaiting those who arouse Kundalini accidentally or prematurely. The most solemn warnings are uttered against attempting anything of the kind until the time is fully ripe and unless under the guidance of a Master or an experienced occultist.

I L I 462.
I L I 463.

Before Kundalini is aroused it is absolutely essential that a definite stage of moral purity be reached and also that the will be strong enough to control the force. Some of the dangers connected with the serpent-fire are purely physical. Its uncontrolled movement often produces intense physical pain, and it may readily tear tissues and even destroy physical life. It may also do permanent injury to vehicles higher than the physical.

One very common effect of arousing it prematurely is that it rushes downwards into the lower centres of the body instead of upwards, resulting in the excitation of the most undesirable passions, which are apt to be intensified to such a degree that it is quite impossible for the man to resist them. In the grip of such a force he is as helpless as a swimmer in the jaws of a shark. Such men become satyrs, monsters of depravity, being at the mercy of a force out of all proportion to the human power of resistance. It is probable that they *I L I* 464. will attain certain supernormal powers, but these will serve only to bring them into contact with sub-human beings with which humanity is intended to hold no commerce, and to escape from this thraldom may take more than one incarnation. There is a school of black magic which purposely uses this power in this way, but the lower force-centres which in this school are used are always left severely alone by followers of the Good Law or White Magic.

The premature unfoldment of Kundalini intensifies also everything in the nature, reaching in fact the lower evil qualities more readily than the good. Ambition, for example, in the mental body is very readily aroused and grows to an inordinate degree. Together *I L I* 465. with great intensification of intellectual power there comes abnormal and satanic pride. The force of Kundalini is no ordinary force, but something resistless. If an uninstructed man has the misfortune to arouse it, he should at once consult some one who fully understands such matters. As the Hathayogapradipika *I L I* 466. says, "It gives liberation to yogis and bondage to fools."

There are some cases where Kundalini wakes spon- *I L I* 467. taneously, so that a dull glow is felt : it may even, though rarely, begin to move of itself. In this case it would probably cause severe pain, as, since the passages are not prepared for it, it would have to clear its way by actually burning up a great deal of etheric dross, a process necessarily painful. In such cases the force *I L I* 468. would usually rush up the interior of the spine, instead of following the spiral course into which the occultist is trained to guide it. An effort of will should be made, if possible, to arrest its upward rush, but if that proves to be impossible, as is most likely, it will probably rush out through the head and escape into the atmosphere, probably doing no harm further than causing a slight weakening. It may also cause a temporary loss of consciousness. The really serious dangers, however, are connected, not with the upward, but with the downward rush.

As already briefly mentioned, the principal function of Kundalini in occult development is to pass through the etheric force-centres and vivify these so that they bring through into the physical consciousness astral experiences. Thus *The Voice of the Silence* teaches that a vivification in this manner of the eyebrows centre enables one to hear the voice of the Master, that is, of *I L I* 469. the Ego or higher self. The explanation of this is that the pituitary body when fully working affords a perfect link between astral and physical consciousness.

The mastery of Kundalini has to be repeated in each incarnation, because in each life the bodies are new, but after it has once been thoroughly achieved, repetition becomes an easy matter.

I L I 469. The formation of the link between the physical consciousness and that of the Ego has its correspondences also at higher levels, meaning for the Ego a link with the consciousness of the Monad, and for the Monad a link with the consciousness of the Logos.

I L I 472. Age does not appear to affect the development of the chakrams by means of Kundalini, but health is a necessity, as only a strong body could endure the strain.

CHAPTER XIV

THE ATOMIC WEB

(See Diagram XIV)

WE have already seen that there is a very close connection between the chakrams in the astral body and
those in the Etheric Double.   Between these two sets

I L I 472-3.

DIAGRAM XIV
THE ATOMIC SHIELD

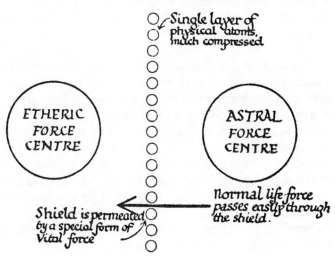

Function of Shield : To prevent astral influences from prematurely
entering physical consciousness.
Ways of injuring the shield :—
(1) Emotional shock, *e.g.*, fear, anger.
(2) Alcohol.
(3) Narcotic drugs, *e.g.*, tobacco.
(4) " Sitting for development."

of centres, and interpenetrating them in a manner not
easy to describe, there is a web or sheath, composed of
a single layer of physical atoms, closely woven, much
compressed, and permeated with a special variety of

F

Prâna. The Prâna which normally comes from the astral into the physical is such that it can pass with perfect ease through the atomic shield, but the latter is an absolute barrier to all other forces which cannot use the atomic matter of both planes.

The shield is thus a protection provided by nature to prevent premature opening up of communication between the astral and physical planes. Were it not for this wise provision, all kinds of astral experiences might pour into the physical consciousness where, in the case of most men, they could be productive of nothing but harm.

I L I I 116.

At any moment an astral entity might introduce forces which an ordinary man would be quite unprepared to meet, and which would be entirely beyond his strength to cope with. A man would be liable to obsession by any astral entity who desired to seize his vehicle.

The atomic shield thus serves as an effective safeguard against these undesirable happenings. It also serves under normal conditions to prevent clear recollection of the sleep life from reaching the physical brain consciousness ; and it accounts for the momentary unconsciousness which always occurs at death. Occasionally the returning astral body succeeds in making a momentary impression on the Etheric Double and dense body, so that when the latter awake there is a touch of vivid memory. This usually quickly vanishes, effort to recall it rendering success more impossible, as each effort sets up physical brain vibrations which tend to overpower the subtler astral vibrations.

M B 51.

It is clear, therefore, that any injury to the shield is a serious disaster. Such injury may occur in several ways. Any great emotional shock, or any strong emotion of an evil character, which produces a kind of explosion in the astral body, may produce such an effect, rending apart the delicate web and, as we say, driving the man mad. A terrible fright may do this, or an outburst of anger.

I L I 474.

Sitting for development, as spiritualists call the

process, may also injure the web and throw open the doors which nature intended to be kept closed.

Certain drugs, notably alcohol and all the narcotics, of which tobacco is one, contain matter which on breaking up volatilises, some of it passing from the physical to the astral state. Students of dietetics, especially those who have studied the effects of toxins, will be interested to learn that even tea and coffee contain the class of material described, though in quantities so small that only after long-continued abuse of them would the effect manifest itself. When this takes place, these constituents rush out through the chakrams in the direction opposite to that for which they are intended, and after doing this repeatedly they injure *I L I* 475. and finally destroy the delicate web.

There are two ways in which this deterioration or destruction may be brought about, according to the type of person concerned and the proportion of the constituents in his etheric and astral bodies. In the first type the rush of volatilising matter actually burns away the web, and thus breaks down nature's barrier.

In the second type the volatile constituents harden the atom, checking and crippling its pulsations, so that it can no longer carry the special form of Prâna which welds it into the web. The web thus becomes as it were ossified, so that instead of too much coming through from one plane to another, we have very little of any kind coming through.

The two types are readily recognisable. In the former case we have instances of delirium tremens, obsession, and certain forms of insanity. In the latter *I L I* 476. case, which is by far the more common, we notice a general deadening of the higher feelings and qualities, resulting in materialism, brutality, animalism, and loss of self-control. It is well known that those who indulge excessively in narcotics, such as tobacco, will persist in their self-indulgence even at the expense of the pain or discomfort of their neighbours. Their finer susceptibilities have to that extent become blunted.

As the consciousness of the ordinary man cannot *I L I* 477.

I L I 478.

normally use atomic matter, either physical or astral, there is normally no possibility of conscious communication between the two planes. As, however, he purifies his vehicles, he becomes able to function in the atomic matter and then is able to carry his consciousness along the direct road from one atomic level to the other. In this case the atomic web fully retains its position and activity, permitting the consciousness to pass from one plane to another, while at the same time fulfilling its purpose of preventing close contact with those lower sub-planes from which many kinds of undesirable influences are liable to come.

The only safe way, therefore, for genuine students of occultism, is not to force in any way the development of psychic powers, but to wait for these to unfold, as they will unfold, in the normal course of evolution. By this way all the benefits will be obtained and the dangers avoided.

CHAPTER XV

BIRTH

It will now be useful to study the Etheric Double in its connection with the birth and death of the physical body

Those who have studied the mechanism of reincarnation will be familiar with the fact that, in the case of the etheric body, a factor comes into play which does not operate in the case of the astral or mental bodies. The Etheric Double is actually built in advance for the incoming Ego, by an elemental which is the joint *I L I I* 442. thought-form of the four Devarājas, each of whom presides over one of the four etheric sub-planes of physical matter. The primary business of this building elemental is to construct the etheric mould into which the physical particles of the new baby-body are to be built.

The form and colour of this elemental vary in dif- *I L II* 447. ferent cases. At first it accurately expresses in shape and size the infant body it has to build ; clairvoyants sometimes see this doll-like little figure hovering about, and afterwards within, the body of the mother, and have occasionally mistaken it for the soul of the coming baby instead of the mould of its physical body.

As soon as the fœtus has grown to the size of the *I L I I* 448. mould, and is ready for birth, the form of the next stage at which it has to aim is unfolded—the size, shape and condition of the body as it is to be, so far as the work of the elemental is concerned, at the time when it proposes to leave it. After the elemental has retired, all further growth of the body is under the control of the Ego himself.

In both these cases the elemental uses itself as the mould. Its colours largely represent the qualities *I L I I* 449.

required in the body it has to build, and its form is also usually that destined for it. As soon as its work is done, there is no power left to hold together its particles and the elemental disintegrates.

I L I I 440.

In determining the quality of etheric matter to be used in building the etheric body, we have two things to consider: first, the type of matter, regarded from the point of view of the seven Rays or *vertical* divisions, and secondly, the quality of matter, regarded from the point of view of its coarseness or fineness, or *horizontal* divisions. The former, the ray-type, is determined by the physical permanent atom, which has the type and sub-type impressed upon it   The latter is determined by the past karma of the man, the building elemental being charged with the production of the type of physical body suited to the man's requirements. The

I L I I 497.

elemental, in fact, consists of that portion of the (prârabda) *karma* of the individual which is to express

I L I I 447.

itself in the physical body. On the selection made by the building elemental depends, for example, whether the body will be naturally clever or stupid, placid or irritable, energetic or lethargic, sensitive or unresponsive. The potentialities of heredity are latent in the maternal ovum and the paternal spermatozoon, and from these the elemental makes his selection according to the requirements of the case.

Although the elemental is in charge of the body from the first, the Ego only comes into contact with his future habitation later, some time before physical birth. If the characteristics the elemental has to impose are few in number, it is able to withdraw early and leave the Ego in full control of the body. Where, however, much time is required to develop the limita-

I L I I 448.

tions needed, the elemental may retain its position until the body is seven years old.

Etheric matter for the infant body is taken from the

J L I I 450.

body of the mother; hence the importance of the latter supplying her body with only the purest materials. Unless the elemental is charged with some special development in the way of features, such as unusual beauty or the reverse, the principal agency at work in this direction will be the thoughts of the mother and the thought-forms which float around her.

The new astral body comes into connection with the *A W* 269. Etheric Double at a very early stage, and exercises considerable influence over its formation, the mental body also working through it upon the nervous organisation.

CHAPTER XVI

DEATH

D A 17.

S P 12.

WE have previously seen that, under certain conditions, the Etheric Double may be separated from the dense body, though it is always connected with it by a thread or cord of etheric matter. At death the double finally withdraws from the dense body and may be seen as a violet mist, gradually condensing into a figure which is the counterpart of the expiring person and attached to the dense body by a glistening thread. This thread or magnetic cord is snapped at the moment of death.

S C 92–3.

As the buddhic life-web, accompanied by Prâna, disentangles itself from dense physical matter at death, it draws itself together in the heart round the permanent atom. The atom, web and Prâna then rise along the secondary Sushumna-nadî into the third ventricle of the brain, thence to the point of junction of the parietal and occipital sutures, and finally out of the body. The life-web remains enshrouding the physical permanent atom, in the causal body, until the time comes for a new physical body to be built.

S S 62.

The withdrawal of the Etheric Double, and with it of course Prâna, destroys the integral unity of the physical body, thus leaving it merely as a collection of independent cells. The life of the separate cells themselves continues, as evidenced by the well-known fact that hairs on a corpse will sometimes continue to grow.

D A 16;
S D I 587.

The moment the Etheric Double withdraws, and consequently Prâna ceases to circulate, the lower lives, *i.e.*, the cells, run rampant and begin to break down the hitherto definitely organised body. The body is thus never more alive than when it is dead : but it is alive in its units, and dead in its totality ; alive as a congeries, dead as an organism. As Eliphas Levi says : " The corpse would not decompose if it were dead ; all the molecules which compose it are living and struggle to separate." (*Isis Unveiled*, I., 480).

When the double finally quits the dense body, it does not go far away but usually floats over it. In this condition it is known as the wraith, and sometimes appears to those with whom it is closely bound up as a cloudy figure, very dully conscious and speechless. Unless disturbed by tumultuous distress or violent emotion, the state of consciousness is dreamy and peaceful.

D A 21.

A W 71.

D A 21.

It is during the withdrawal of the double, as well as afterwards, that the whole of the man's past life passes swiftly in review before the Ego, every forgotten nook and corner of the memory yielding up its secrets, picture after picture, event after event. In these few seconds the Ego lives over again his whole life, seeing his successes and failures, loves and hatreds : he perceives the predominant tendency of the whole, and the ruling thought of the life asserts itself, marking the region in which the chief part of the post-mortem life will be spent. As the *Kaushitakopanishat* describes it, at death Prâna gathers everything together and, withdrawing from the body, hands everything onwards to the Knower, who is the receptacle of all.

M B 22.

D A 22.

A W 110.

S S 63.

This stage is usually followed by a brief period of peaceful unconsciousness, due to the withdrawal of the etheric matter and its entanglement with the astral body, thus preventing the man from functioning either in the physical or the astral world. Some men shake themselves free from the etheric envelope in a few moments : others rest within it for hours, days, or even weeks, though usually the process does not take longer than a few hours.

A W 112;
I L I I 34;
T B T 131.

As the days pass, the higher principles gradually disengage themselves from the double, and the latter then becomes in its turn an etheric corpse, which remains near the dense one, both disintegrating together. These etheric wraiths are often seen in churchyards, sometimes as violet or bluish-white mists or

S P 13;
D A 23;
T N P 79;
A P 53.

lights, but often presenting an unpleasant appearance as they pass through various stages of decomposition.

A W 112.

One of the great advantages of cremation is that by destroying the dense physical body, the etheric body also loses its nidus and so rapidly disintegrates.

I L I I 21-2.

If a man is so misguided as to wish to cling to physical life, and even to his own corpse, the preservation of the dead body, either by burial or embalming, offers a distinct temptation to him to do so, and immensely facilitates his unfortunate purpose. Cremation entirely prevents any attempt at partial and unnatural temporary reunion of the principles. In addition, there are certain unpleasant forms of black magic, fortunately rare in

H S I 336 ;
D A 24.

Western countries at least, which make use of the decaying physical body; the etheric body of a dead person may also be similarly used in a variety of ways.

H S I 337.

All of these possibilities are avoided by the wholesome practice of cremation. It is quite impossible for a dead person to feel the effects of the fire on his discarded body, for, so long as it *is* death, the astral and etheric matter have been completely separated from the dense physical.

H S I 335.

Although it is quite impossible for a dead person to get back entirely into his dead body, yet, in the case of one who knows of nothing beyond purely physical life and is crazy with fear at being entirely cut off from it, it is possible for him, in his frantic effort to keep in touch with physical life, to get hold of the etheric matter of the discarded body and drag it about with him. This may be the cause of considerable suffering, entirely unnecessary, and easily avoided by the practice of cremation.

I L I I 34.

In the case of people who cling desperately to physical existence, the astral body cannot altogether separate from the etheric, and they awaken still sur-

I L I I 35.

rounded by etheric matter. The condition is very unpleasant, as such a person would be shut out from the astral world by the shell of etheric matter, and at the same time the loss of physical sense-organs prevents him from coming fully into touch with earth-life. Conse-

quently he drifts about, lonely, dumb and terrified, in a
thick and gloomy fog, unable to hold intercourse with
either plane.

In process of time the etheric shell wears out, in spite *I L I I* 37.
of his struggles, though usually not until after he has
suffered intensely. Kindly people among the dead, and *I L I I* 36.
others, endeavour to help the class of person described,
but seldom with success.

Sometimes a person in this condition may endeavour *I L I I* 37.
to get into touch once again with the physical plane
through a medium, though usually the medium's
" spirit-guides " sternly forbid them access, knowing
that the medium runs the risk of being obsessed or
maddened. Occasionally an unconscious medium—
usually a sensitive young girl—may be seized upon, but *I L I I* 38.
the attempt can be successful only if the girl's Ego has
weakened his hold on his vehicles by indulging in
undesirable thoughts or passions. Occasonally also a
human soul wandering in this grey world may succeed
in partially obsessing an animal, those most commonly *I L I I* 41.
seized upon being the less developed—cattle, sheep or
swine, though cats, dogs or monkeys may also be used
in this way. This appears to be the modern, *i.e.*, Fifth *I L I I* 42.
Race, substitute for the awful life of the vampire, found
in Fourth Race peoples. Once entangled with an animal,
it is possible to disentangle oneself only gradually and *I L I I* 40.
by considerable effort, extending probably for many
days. Freedom usually comes only at the death of the
animal, and even then there remains an astral entangle- *I L II* 41.
ment to shake off.

CHAPTER XVII

HEALING

We have already seen that a man in vigorous health is continually throwing off from his body vital emanations which may be absorbed by others. In this way the latter will be strengthened, and minor illnesses may be cured, or, at least, recovery expedited.

As, however, the currents of Prâna are amenable to the will, it is possible for a man consciously to direct the streams of vitality which pour out of him, as well as greatly to augment their natural flow. By directing the currents on to a patient who is depleted of strength, owing to the fact that his spleen is not doing its work properly, considerable help towards recovery may be given, the additional vitality poured in by the healer keeping the patient's bodily machinery working until it is sufficiently recovered to manufacture supplies of Prâna for itself.

The healing of the weak by the strong may thus be achieved, in certain cases, merely by physical proximity, the process being either entirely unconscious and automatic, or it may be assisted and expedited to almost any extent by conscious effort. Much benefit may often be given merely by pouring into the patient copious streams of vitality, which will flood the patient's system with vitalising energy ; or the operator may direct the flow to the particular portion of the body which is out of health. Merely to increase the circulation of Prâna is sufficient to cure many minor diseases. All nervous diseases imply a jangled condition of the Etheric Double, and that is also the cause of digestive troubles and sleeplessness. Headaches are usually caused by congestion, either of blood or of the vital fluid, sometimes called magnetism. A strong current directed by

H S I 73.

I L I I 179.

S G O 186.

S G O 186.

S G O 187.
I L I I 179.

the healer through the head of the sufferer will wash *H S I I* 217.
away the congested matter and the headache will
disappear.

These methods are comparatively simple and by no
means difficult to apply, though a skilful healer, especially if clairvoyant, can improve on them enormously.
One such improvement, which demands some know- *S G O* 187.
ledge of anatomy and physiology, is to make a mental
picture of the diseased organ, and then image it as it
should be in health. The strong thought will mould
etheric matter into the desired form, which will help
nature to build up new tissues much more rapidly than
would otherwise be possible.

A still more thorough method is to create the organ *S C* 430.
in mental matter : then to build into it astral matter :
then to densify it with etheric matter : and finally to
build into the mould gases, liquids and solids, utilising
materials available in the body and supplying from
outside any deficiencies.

A methodical and effective way to set to work to *R M* 81.
heal magnetically is as follows: The patient assumes
a comfortable position, either sitting or lying down, and *R M* 156.
is instructed to relax as thoroughly as possible. A very
convenient method is for the patient to sit in an easy
chair, with solid flat arms, the operator sitting sideways
on the arms and thus being slightly above the patient.
The operator then makes passes with his hands over the
patient's body, or over that portion of it which he proposes to treat magnetically, making an effort of will to
withdraw from the patient the congested or diseased
etheric matter. These passes may be made without
actually touching the patient, though it is often an *R M* 82.
assistance to lay the whole hand on the skin gently and
lightly. After each pass the operator must take care
to throw off from himself the etheric matter he has
withdrawn, otherwise some of it may remain in his own *S G O* 162.
system and he may presently find himself suffering from *R M* 83.
a complaint similar to that of which he has cured his
patient. Many cases of this kind are on record ; thus,
an operator may remove pain from a patient's tooth, or

elbow, only to find himself presently suffering from toothache or pain in the elbow. In some cases, where repeated treatments are given, an operator who neglects to throw off the diseased matter which he has extracted may make himself seriously ill and even become a chronic sufferer.

R M 87.

A. P. Sinnett gives a curious case of a lady who was cured of chronic rheumatism and then went to live in a part of Europe other than that in which the mesmeric operator resided. Four years afterwards the operator died, and the old rheumatic trouble at once returned to the lady with its former virulence. In this case it would seem that the unhealthy magnetism which the operator had withdrawn from the patient, but had not destroyed, had for years been hanging around the aura of the operator and, on his death, had at once flown back to where it originally belonged.

R M 162.

Usually it is sufficient to jerk the hands sharply downwards and away from oneself, or the magnetism may be thrown into a basin of water, the water afterwards of course being thrown away. The process may be assisted after this preliminary portion of the treatment is completed by washing the hands in water before commencing the next and more positive part of the treatment.

R M 85.

It is also said to be possible to direct the unhealthy magnetism to certain classes of elementals, where it will find its appropriate sphere. The Bible parable of the herd of swine may well be an allegorical description of the process. It would certainly seem to be preferable for something of this kind to be done than for the unhealthy magnetism to be left floating about near the aura either of the healer or of others who may happen to be near.

A slight variation of the above method, especially useful in the case of local congestion, is to place the hands, one on either side of the affected area, and to direct a stream of cleansing magnetism from the right hand towards the left hand, this magnetism driving out the patient's congested material.

The way having thus been prepared, the next stage is to pour into the patient one's own magnetic fluid and Prâna. This is done by making similar passes, though this time with a strong effort of will to pour out one's own force into the patient. This, as before, may be done by means of long sweeping passes over the whole body, or by shorter passes over a special area : or, again, the two hands may be used, the current being passed from the right hand to the left, through the area that is being treated.

The student will readily recognise the desirability of the healer being himself perfectly healthy, because otherwise he is liable to pour into the patient some of his own unhealthy magnetism.

It should be noted that in magnetic healing clothing is somewhat of a barrier, silk being in this respect the worst. The minimum possible, therefore, according to circumstances, should be worn by the patient. *R M* 163.

From the fact that certain forms of insanity are due to defects in the etheric brain, its particles not corresponding perfectly with the denser physical particles and thus being unable to bring through properly vibrations from the higher vehicles, we may surmise that such cases might lend themselves to cure by magnetic treatment. *I L I* 482.

There are, of course, other methods of affecting the etheric body, because the connection between mental, astral and etheric bodies is so close that any one of the three may affect any of the others. *S G O* 187.

Generally speaking, it may be said that anything which promotes physical health also reacts favourably on the higher vehicles. Unused muscles, for example, not only tend to deteriorate, but produce a congestion of magnetism : this means a weak place in the Etheric Double, through which unpleasant germs, such as those of infection, may enter. *H S I I* 29-30.

Similarly, mental or astral ill-health will almost surely, sooner or later, be reflected as physical disease. A person who is astrally " fussy," *i.e.*, who allows his astral body to fritter away his strength on petty little

emotions, troubles and worries, not only is apt to produce unpleasant and disturbing effects on the astral
bodies of other sensitive persons, but frequently the
perpetual astral disturbance reacts through the etheric
upon the dense physical body, and all sorts of nervous
diseases are produced.

Nearly all nerve-troubles, for example, are the direct
result of unnecessary worry and emotion, and would
soon disappear if the patient could be taught to hold his
vehicles still and peaceful.

Magnetic healing blends almost imperceptibly into
mesmerism, which we shall therefore now proceed to
examine.

CHAPTER XVIII

THE student should recognise the perfectly clear and definite distinction between hypnotism and mesmerism. Hypnotism, derived from the Greek *hupnos*, meaning sleep, stands literally for the art of putting to sleep. It usually results from a nervous paralysis brought about by a slight strain either to the nerves of the eye or in some other way. It is not, in itself, an injurious state to be in, though it may of course be turned to ends either good or bad. It frequently makes the subject insensible to pain, and it may give the system a rest which may be highly beneficial. It is primarily a self-induced condition : its main result is that it usually places the subject to a greater or lesser extent under the control of the operator who, within certain limits which vary according to the nature and character of the subject and the degree of the hypnosis as well as the power and skill of the operator, may be compelled to do what the operator wishes.

S G O 151.

N M 117.

Mesmerism depends upon quite a different principle. The word itself is derived from Frederick Mesmer (1734–1815), a doctor of Vienna, who, towards the end of the eighteenth century, discovered that he could effect cures by means of influences proceeding from the hand, to which he gave the name " animal magnetism." The essence of Mesmerism is that the operator drives out or forces back the patient's own magnetism or vital fluid, and replaces it with his own fluid. The natural effect of this is that the patient loses all power of feeling in that portion of his body from which his own fluid has been expelled. We have previously seen that the power of feeling depends on the transmission of contacts to the astral centres, through the matter of the

H S I 82.
N M 114.

R M 97.
S G O 159.

G

Etheric Double. When, therefore, the etheric matter is removed, the connection between the dense physical body and the astral body is broken, and consequently there can be no sensation experienced.

M V 130.

The withdrawal of the vital fluid does not in any way interfere with the circulation of the blood, for the portion of the body concerned remains warm.

It is thus possible to drive out a patient's own etheric matter from, say, an arm or a leg, so that complete anæsthesia in the limb results. The mesmeric process being in such a case purely local, the patient will retain full normal consciousness in the brain : all that happens is that a local anæsthetic has been applied to the limb concerned. Under such mesmeric anæsthesia surgical operations, both major and minor, have been

R M 47.

performed. Perhaps the best-known collection of such operations is recorded in the book *Mesmerism in India*, first published in 1842, by Dr. Esdaile. Another surgeon, one Dr. Elliotson, also performed large numbers of operations under mesmeric anæsthesia in London

N M 115.

about three-quarters of a century ago. At this time chloroform was unknown, and every operating room was a torture chamber. Graphic and interesting accounts of the work of these two pioneers may be found in *The Rationale of Mesmerism*, by A. P. Sinnett, a book strongly recommended to the student.

The mesmeric process may be pushed further, to the

R M 99.
H S I 82.

extent of driving out the subject's own magnetic fluid from the brain and replacing it by that of the operator. In this case, the subject entirely loses control of his own body and the control passes to the operator, who can then make the subject's body do what the operator wishes.

S G O 163.
R M 103.

An interesting consequence of replacing a subject's magnetic fluid by that of the operator is that a stimulus applied to the operator may appear to be felt by the subject, or, on the other hand, a stimulus applied to the subject may be felt by the operator.

S G O 164.

Thus, for example, suppose that an arm has been mesmerised, the subject's own magnetic fluid being replaced by that of the operator. Then if the operator's hand be pricked, the subject may receive the feeling, owing to the fact that the nerve-ether of the operator has been connected up to the subject's brain : the subject, therefore, receiving the message from the operator's nerve-ether, supposes it to have come from his own nerve-ether and so responds accordingly. This phenomenon is usually known as magnetic sympathy, and many cases may be read of in the literature of the subject.

It is not essential to make passes with the hands in order to mesmerise. The only use of the hands is to concentrate the fluid, and perhaps to help the imagination of the operator, anything which assists the imagination making easier that belief upon which the action of the will so largely depends. A skilful mesmerist, however, can manage quite well without any passes whatever, achieving his results merely by looking at his subject and using his will. *S G O* 162.

It would appear that the etheric mechanism of the body consists of two distinct divisions, the one unconscious and connected with the sympathetic, the other conscious or voluntary, and connected with the cerebrospinal system, and that it is possible to mesmerise the latter, but not the former. A mesmerist would not, therefore, usually be able to interfere with the ordinary vital processes of a patient's body, such as breathing or the circulation of the blood. *R M* 98.

This may, perhaps, be the explanation of the statement in *Theosophy* that Prâna exists in two main forms in the physical body : energising Prâna in the Etheric Double, and Automatic Prâna in the dense body. *T* 25.

As in the case of magnetic healing, it is obviously eminently desirable that a mesmerist should be physically healthy. For a healer or magnetiser pours into the patient not only Prâna, but also his own emanations, and in this way it is possible for the operator to convey physical disease to the subject. Further, as astral and mental matter are also thrown into the subject, moral and mental diseases may likewise be transferred. *O S D* 463.

H S I 82.

O S D 463.

For similar reasons a mesmerist may thus, even unconsciously, gain great influence over his subject— a far greater power than is generally known. Any quality of heart or mind possessed by the mesmerist is very readily transferred to the subject, hence the avenues of possible danger in this respect are apparent.

Cl 165.

Mesmerism purely for curative purposes, by those who understand what they are doing and can be trusted not to abuse their powers, has much to be said for it ; but mesmerism for other purposes is distinctly not advisable.

S C 434.

An advantage possessed by mesmerism over healing of disease by will is that when will-forces are poured down into the physical, there is a danger of driving the disease back into the subtler vehicles from which it came, thus inhibiting the final working out to the physical plane of evil which has its origin in mind and emotion. Curative mesmerism is free from this danger.

I L 172.
S G O 108.

An interesting example of magnetic or mesmeric healing is the Buddhist Paritta or Pirit ceremony (meaning literally " blessings "), in which the monks sit in a circle or hollow square and hold in their hands a rope about as thick as a clothes line, from which strings run to a large pot of water. Relays of monks recite texts from the scriptures for many days continuously, keeping clearly in their minds the will to bless. The water becomes very highly charged with magnetism, and is then distributed to the people, or a sick man may hold a thread connected with the rope.

R M 70.

It may be noted, in passing, that it is possible to mesmerise plants and procure specific and distinct results in stimulation of their growth. There are probably very few who practise this consciously, at least in Western countries, though the fact that some persons have a " lucky hand " with plants, flowers, etc., may perhaps be partially explained on the lines indicated. A more common cause, however, of such phenomena has to do with the composition of the

A W 86 ;
H S I I 320.

etheric and other bodies and the relationship of the

person to the elementals, the most friendly to him being those whose element is preponderant in his vehicles.

Nature-spirits, possessing little sense of responsibility and wills not strongly developed, can usually readily be dominated mesmerically, and can then be employed in many ways to carry out the will of the magician : so long as the tasks given to them are within their powers they will be faithfully and surely executed.

S G O 199.

It is also possible to mesmerise persons who have recently died and who are still hovering close about us in their astral bodies.

S G O 200.

CHAPTER XIX

SHELLS AND SHIELDS

THERE are certain circumstances in which it is both permissible and desirable to form either a shell or a shield of etheric matter, to protect oneself or other people from unpleasant influences of various kinds.

H S I 460.
Thus, for example, in a mixed crowd there is quite likely to be present some physicial magnetism distasteful, if not positively injurious, to a student of occultism.

H S I 461.
Some persons, also, being themselves low in vitality, have the faculty, usually unconscious, of depleting others in their vicinity of their stores of Prâna. Provided these vampire-like people took from others only those etheric particles which are normally expelled from the body as not needed, no harm would be done, but often the suction is so intense that the whole circulation of Prâna in the victim is hastened, the rose-coloured particles also being drawn out of the system

H S I 462.
before their Prânic content has been assimilated by their owner. A capable vampire can thus drain a person of all his strength in a few minutes.

The vampire is not appreciably benefited by the vitality of which he has robbed others, because his own system tends to dissipate what he acquires without proper assimilation. A person in this condition needs mesmeric treatment, strictly limited quantities of Prâna being supplied to him, until the elasticity of his etheric double is restored, so that both the suction and

H S I 463.
the leakage cease. The leakage of vitality takes place through every pore of the body rather than through any one portion of it.

H S I 464.
In certain abnormal cases another entity may attempt to seize and obsess the physical bodies of others. Or, again, it may be necessary to sleep,

e.g., in a railway carriage, in close physical proximity with people of the vampire type or whose emanations are coarse and undesirable ; or the student may have to visit persons or places where disease is rampant. *H S I* 465.

Some people are so sensitive that they are apt to reproduce in their own bodies the symptoms of others who are weak or diseased ; others, again, suffer considerably from the incessant play of the multiplex vibrations in a noisy city. *H S I* 466. *H S I* 467.

In all these cases an etheric shell may be utilised with advantage to protect oneself. It is important to note, however, that an etheric shell which keeps *out* etheric matter will also keep it *in*, and that therefore one's own etheric emanations, many of which are poisonous, will be kept within the shell.

The shell is made by an effort of will and imagination. It may be done in two ways. Either the periphery of the etheric aura, which follows the shape of and is slightly larger than the physical body, may be densified, or an ovoid shell of etheric matter may be manufactured out of the surrounding atmosphere. The latter is preferable, though it demands a far greater exertion of the will and a more definite knowledge of the way in which physical matter is moulded by it. *H S I* 466.

Students who wish to guard their physical bodies during sleep by means of an etheric shell must be careful to make the latter of etheric, not astral, matter. A case is recorded of a student who made this mistake, with the consequence that the physical body was left entirely unprotected, while he himself floated away in an impenetrable astral shell which permitted nothing to pass either to or from the consciousness imprisoned within. *H S I* 469.

The formation of an etheric shell before going to sleep may be of assistance in helping the experiences of the Ego to come through into the waking consciousness by preventing the thoughts which are always floating in the etheric world, and constantly bombarding the vehicles, from entering into the sleeping etheric *D* 67 *&* 30.

brain and becoming there mixed up with the thoughts of that etheric brain itself.

T 27;
S C 136.

The etheric part of the brain, being the playground of the creative imagination, takes an active part in dreams, especially those caused by impressions from outside, or from any internal pressure from the cerebral vessels. Its dreams are usually dramatic, for it draws on the accumulated contents of the physical brain, and arranges, dissociates, and recombines these after its own fancies, thus creating the lower world of dream.

D 30.

The best method of remaining, whilst awake, practically impervious to the impingement of thought from without is to keep the brain fully employed instead of leaving it idle, the door wide open for the streams of inconsequent chaos to pour into it.

D 32.

In sleep the etheric part of the brain is of course even more at the mercy of outside thought-currents. By the means suggested above the student should be able to keep himself free from such troubles.

H S I 467.

In some cases it is not necessary to make a shell to surround the whole body, but merely a small local shield to guard oneself against a special contact.

H S I 468.

Thus some sensitive people suffer acutely merely from shaking hands with others. In such cases a temporary shield of etheric matter may be formed, by an effort of will and imagination, which will completely protect the hand and arm from the entry of a single particle charged with undesirable magnetism.

A P 122.

Similar shields are used for protection against fire, though for this purpose a far greater knowledge of practical magic is needed. Such shields of etheric matter, the thinnest layer of which can be so manipulated as to be absolutely impervious to heat, may be spread over the hands, the feet, or over the hot stones or other substances used in the fire-walking ceremonies still practised in certain parts of the world. This phenomenon is occasionally seen at spiritual séances, the sitters being enabled to handle red-hot coals with impunity.

H S I 466.

It will, of course, be recognised that the shells and

shields we have been speaking about are purely etheric, and therefore have no effect in keeping off astral or mental influences, for which purpose shells of the material of those planes would have to be employed; with these, however, we are not here concerned.

CHAPTER XX

MEDIUMSHIP

A W 70.   A MEDIUM is an abnormally organised person in whom dislocation of the etheric and dense bodies easily occurs. The Etheric Double, when extruded, largely supplies the physical basis for " materialisations."

A P 117.   Such materialised forms are usually strictly confined to the immediate neighbourhood of the medium, the matter of which they are composed being subject to an attraction which is constantly drawing it back to the body from which it came, so that if kept away from the medium too long the figure collapses, the matter which composes it instantly rushing back to its source.

A P 118.   Such forms are able to exist for a few moments only amidst the intense vibrations of brilliant light.

M B 31.   The condition of mediumship is, on the whole, dangerous, and fortunately comparatively rare : it gives rise to much nervous strain and disturbance. When the Etheric Double is extruded, the double itself is rent in twain ; the whole of it could not be separated from the dense body without causing death, since the life-force, or Prâna, cannot circulate without the presence of etheric matter. Even the partial withdrawal of the double produces lethargy in the dense body and almost suspends the vital activities : this dangerous condition is usually followed by extreme exhaustion (see Chap. I., page 5).

I L I I 176.   The terrible drain on the vitality, set up by a withdrawal of the means by which the Prâna is circulated, is the reason why mediums are so often in a state of collapse after a séance, and also why so many mediums eventually become drunkards, stimulants being taken in order to satisfy the terrible craving for support caused by the sudden loss of strength.

Sir William Crookes, on page 41 of his *Researches*, writes : " After witnessing the painful state of nervous and bodily prostration in which some of these experiments have left Mr. Home—after seeing him lying in an almost fainting condition on the floor, pale and speechless—I could scarcely doubt that the evolution of psychic force is accompanied by a corresponding drain on vital force."

O S 382.

The condition closely resembles the shock which follows a surgical operation.

At a spiritual séance a clairvoyant can see the Etheric Double oozing usually out of the left side of the medium, though sometimes from the whole surface of the body, and it is this which often appears as the " materialised spirit," easily moulded into various shapes by the thoughts of the sitters, and gaining strength and vitality as the medium sinks into a deep trance. Usually, of course, this takes place without any conscious effort on the part of the sitters : it may, however, be achieved deliberately. Thus, H. P. Blavatsky stated that during the remarkable phenomena at the Eddy homestead she deliberately moulded the " spirit " form which appeared into various likenesses, these being seen by the sitters present.

S P 10.

O S D 378; *S P* 10.

S P 11.

Although etheric matter, moulded into such " spirit " forms, is invisible to ordinary sight, it may nevertheless be able to affect a photographic plate, the latter being sensitive to certain wave-lengths of light which leave the human eye unaffected. This is the rationale of the many cases on record where " spirit-forms " have appeared on the negative of an ordinary photographic portrait.

N M 132–3; *A P* 118.

In addition to the matter of the Etheric Double of the medium, it frequently happens at séances that etheric matter is withdrawn also from the bodies of the sitters : hence the lassitude frequently felt by those who attend such séances.

I L I I 177; *O S D* 394.

M V 131.

It is only in conditions of perfect passivity that much matter can be withdrawn from the physical body without danger to life. Although the medium is usually

O S D 383.

conscious all the time in the background, yet any attempt to assert the individuality, or to think connectedly, immediately weakens the materialised form, or brings it back to the " cabinet." A sudden shock or disturbance, or any attempt to seize the " spirit form," is apt to be in the highest degree dangerous and may even result in death.

I L I I 177.
In addition to the extrusion of etheric matter, in many cases dense physical matter, probably chiefly gases and liquids, is also removed at the same time from the body of the medium. Many cases are on record where, during a materialisation, the body of the medium

O S D 377.
shrivelled perceptibly, the shrunken, wizened appearance of the face being said to be singularly ghastly and unpleasant to see. By actual weighing, the physical body of the medium has been found to be as much as 40 pounds less than normal, whilst the weight of the materialised form has been found to be at least as much as the diminution of the medium's weight, and usually more than this, presumably owing to the extraction of

M B 32.
some dense matter from the bodies of the sitters. In one well-known case a materialised form carried the diminished body of the medium—Mr. Eglinton.

I L I I 175.
To an astral entity, who wishes to " manifest " himself or to produce some phenomenon on the physical plane, a medium serves the purpose of providing the necessary etheric matter, which acts as an intermediary to convey the astral forces into physical matter.

I L I I 6.
A somewhat similar process takes place when a dead drunkard, hovering about a gin-shop, draws round himself a veil of etheric matter, in order that he may absorb the odour of the alcohol for which he craves. Being unable to smell alcohol in the same way as we do, he tries to induce others to become drunk, so that he may be able partially to enter their physical bodies and obsess them, thus once more directly experiencing the taste and other sensations he so ardently desires.

I L I I 175.
Sometimes only sufficient etheric matter is withdrawn from a medium to produce an etheric hand, or even just sufficient of the fingers to hold a pencil and

write, or to enable " raps " to be made, objects to be
overturned or moved, and so forth. Usually, etheric
matter, as well as dense physical matter, is withdrawn
from the medium and utilised so as to cover an astral
shape just sufficiently to make the latter visible to the
sitters, the form seen thus not being solid but merely
a thin film.

" Spirit " drapery, however, so usual at séances. is   *O S D* 389.
frequently made from the clothing of the medium or of
a sitter. The texture may be quite coarse, or exceedingly
fine, finer in fact than any product of Eastern looms.
Occasionally such drapery may be removed from the
séance room, sometimes lasting for years, at other
times fading away in an hour or so, or even in a few
minutes.

There can be no question that, except possibly in
very rare cases, and where every possible precaution is
taken, the practice of mediumship is harmful, and may
be exceedingly dangerous. Nevertheless, it must be
admitted that by its means large numbers of people
have acquired knowledge of, or belief in, the reality of
the unseen world and of the continuance of life after
death. On the other hand, it may be urged that such
knowledge or such belief could have been secured in
other and less harmful ways.

A trained occultist, for example, connected with any   *I L I I* 178;
school of " white magic," would never interfere with   *A P* 119.
the Etheric Double of any man in order to produce a
materialisation ; nor would he disturb his own if he
wished to make himself visible at a distance. He would
simply condense and build into and around his astral
body a sufficient quantity of the surrounding ether to
materialise it, and hold it in that form by an effort of
will as long as he needed it.

Most spirit " guides " are well aware of the dangers   *O S D* 385.
to which their mediums are exposed, and take every
precaution in their power to protect the mediums.
Even the " spirits " themselves may occasionally suffer
when, for example, a materialised form is struck or
wounded, owing to the intimate connection established

between the etheric matter of the materialised form and the astral matter of the " spirit's " body.

It is, of course. true that no physical weapon could affect an astral body, but an injury to a materialised form may be transmitted to the astral body by the phenomenon known as " repercussion."

O S D 394. Owing to the fact that during a materialisation matter may be borrowed from all the sitters present as well as from the medium, a considerable intermixture of such matter may take place, and consequently undesirable qualities or vices in any one of the sitters are liable to react upon the others and most of all upon the medium, who is most drawn upon and is almost certainly the most sensitive person present. Nicotine and alcoholic poisoning appear to be especially liable to produce unpleasant effects in this manner.

S I 20. Mediums of low type inevitably attract eminently undesirable astral entities, who may reinforce their own vitality at the expense of medium and sitters. Such a " spook " may even attach itself to any one present, who is of low development, with deplorable results.

I L I 493. Cases are also known where some outside entity, either incarnate or excarnate, has seized upon the body of a sleeping man and used it, perhaps in sleep-walking, for his own ends. This would be most likely to happen with a person who is mediumistic.

CHAPTER XXI

THE WORK OF DR. WALTER J. KILNER

(*N.B.*—All the marginal references in this chapter
are to *The Human Atmosphere*)

In a book called *The Human Atmosphere* (1911), Dr.
W. J. Kilner describes the investigations he has made
on the human aura by means of coloured screens. Dr.
Kilner's main principles and discoveries are summarised
in this chapter. For further details, especially of the
manner of using the screens, the reader is referred to
the book mentioned.

It is interesting to note that Dr. Kilner expressly V, 2.
disclaims all clairvoyant power and did not even read
accounts of the aura until over sixty of his patients had
been examined. He claims that his methods are purely
physical and can be employed with success by any one
who takes the necessary pains.

The screens are thin, flat glass cells, containing 5.
dicyanin dyes in alcohol. Various colours are employed,
for different purposes, such as dark and light carmine,
blue, green and yellow.

The operator looks through a dark screen at the light 11.
for half a minute or longer, and then at the patient
through a pale screen, when he finds he is able to perceive the aura. Use of the screens appears to affect the 7.
eyes, at first temporarily and later permanently, so that
after a time the operator is able to perceive the aura
even without the screens. Great care, however, is
advised in using the screens, as the eyes tend to become
very painful.

A dull diffused light, from one direction only, pre- 8.
ferably from behind the observer, should be used,
generally sufficient to enable the body to be seen dis- 9.

10.

tinctly. A dead black background is usually necessary, though for some observations a white one is required. The person being observed should be about 12 inches in front of the background, to avoid shadows and other optical illusions.

114.

122.

In addition to the coloured screens, Dr. Kilner has employed another ingenious method of investigating the aura, which he terms that of Complementary Colours. A band of colour, 2 in. by ¾ in., fairly well illuminated, is looked at steadily for thirty to sixty seconds. This has the effect of fatiguing the powers of the eye to perceive that particular olour, and in addition, the eyes are found to become abnormally sensitive to other colours. When, then, the gaze is transferred to the patient, a belt or band of the complementary colour is seen, the same size and shape as the original strip: this " spectre " persists for some little time. In practice it is found that colour changes in the auras produce the effect of changing the appearance of the C.C. band. By this means, in skilful hands, a number of facts about the aura can be ascertained, which, by means of the screens alone, would remain undetected. The colours employed by Dr. Kilner are :—

1. Gamboge having a C.C. Prussian Blue.
2. Antwerp Blue having a C.C. Gamboge.
3. Carmine having a C.C. Transparent Emerald Green.
4. Emerald Green having a C.C. Carmine.

21. 66.

The aura is observed to consist of three distinct parts, called by Dr. Kilner :

(1) The Etheric Double.
(2) The Inner Aura.
(3) The Outer Aura.

66.

67.

The *Etheric Double* appears through the screens as a dark band adjacent to and following exactly the contours of the body. Its width is uniform throughout and is usually from one-sixteenth to three-sixteenths of an inch. It varies in size with different people, and also

with the same person under altered conditions. It
appears to be quite transparent and distinctly striated,   75.
with very delicate lines of a beautiful rose colour, these
appearing to tint the portions between the striations.
The rose colour certainly contains more blue than there
is in carmine. It seems probable that the lines are self-   76.
luminous. Up to the present no attributes or changes in
the Etheric Double have been found which are likely to
be a help in diagnosis.

The *Inner Aura* commences from the outer edge of   21.
the Etheric Double, though frequently it appears to
touch the body itself. It is usually of a uniform width   79.
of 2 to 4 inches throughout, though sometimes slightly
narrower down the limbs, and follows the contours of
the body. It is relatively wider in children than in
adults. Its structure is granular, the granules being   21, 80.
exceedingly fine and so arranged as to appear striated.
The striæ are parallel to one another, being at right
angles to the body, and in bundles, the longest in the
centre and the shortest on the outside, with a rounded
margin. The bundles are massed together, thus creating a crenated outline of the aura. The striæ have not
been observed to possess any colour. In ill-health they   81.
are less apparent.

The Inner Aura is the densest portion of the aura
proper. It is usually more distinctly marked and   64.
broader in persons in robust physical health.   223.

The *Outer Aura* commences from the outer edge of   21.
the Inner Aura and, unlike the Inner Aura, varies in
size considerably. Round the head it extends usually   15.
about 2 inches beyond the shoulders : by the sides and
back of the trunk it is about 4 or 5 inches wide, in front
of the body it is a little narrower. It follows closely the
contours of the body, being sometimes a little narrower
down the lower limbs. Around the arms it corresponds
to that encircling the legs, but is generally broader
round the hands and frequently projects a long distance   82.
from the finger tips. The outline is not absolutely
sharp, but gradually vanishes into space. The Outer   83.
Aura appears structureless and non-luminous. The   226.

H

inner portion of the Outer Aura has larger granules than the outer portions, the different sizes graduating imperceptibly into one another.

15.
14. The auras of boys and girls up to the age of about twelve or thirteen appear similar except that the texture of the female aura is usually finer than that of the male. From adolescence onwards the male and female auras become distinctive : in both, however, considerable individual peculiarities occur. The female aura is usually much wider at the sides of the body, the maximum width being at the waist, and it is also wider at the back than at the front, the widest part being at the small of the back, where frequently it bulges out.

16.

18.
64. Dr Kilner considers that a form approximating to an egg-shaped oval is the most perfect, deviations from this being due to undevelopment. Fineness and transparency may be considered indications of a higher type of aura.

59. Children have auras relatively broader in proportion to their height than adults.

28. Children also, especially males, have an Inner Aura almost as wide as the Outer, so that it may be difficult to differentiate the two.

63.
64. Persons of intelligence usually have larger auras than those of low intellect. This is especially marked round the head. The more grey there is in the aura, the more dull or mentally affected is the owner.

82. Sometimes an exceedingly faint haze can be seen extending outwards a very long distance beyond the Outer Aura. This has been observed only where the aura is unusually extensive, and it appears probable that it is a continuation of the Outer Aura. Dr. Kilner calls this the Ultra-Outer Aura.

83. Bright patches, rays or streams have been observed, emanating from various parts of the body. Sometimes they appear and disappear rapidly, at other times they persist. Patches never seem to be coloured : rays are usually colourless, though occasionally tinted with different hues. Where they occur the aura usually becomes denser. There are three varieties :—

86.

First.—Rays or Patches, lighter than the surrounding 84. aura, entirely separated from but close to the body, appearing in and enveloped by the aura itself. In their most common form they are elongated, their long axes parallel with the body. Their sides are usually distinct, exactly coincident with the edge of the Inner Aura, but the ends, usually contracted and less bright, often fade into the adjacent aura.

The Inner Aura within the Ray usually, but not 85. always, loses its striated appearance, and becomes granular. The longer the Ray persists the coarser become the granules.

Second.—Rays emanating from one part of the body 86. and running to another part, not very distant. These Rays are usually the most brilliant. They may be perceived running, *e.g.*, from the body to an arm, or, if the arm be bent, from the arm-pit to the wrist.

If the observer holds his hand near the patient, the 104. auras of both almost invariably become brighter locally, and in a short time a complete Ray will be formed between the hand and the nearest part of the patient. Such Rays are formed more easily between points than between surfaces.

In one instance a Ray from the hand of one person to 87. that of another was a bright yellow, changing to a liquid ruby colour.

Third.—Rays projecting at right angles from the 87. body into space, brighter than and as far as, or even beyond, the Outer Aura. The sides of the Rays are usually, though not always, parallel, and rarely fan-shaped ; the ends become pointed and fade away, especially when issuing from the tips of the fingers.

Rays have never been observed other than straight. 88. Their normal direction is perpendicular to the body, but they may take any direction, as, for example, when flowing from the tips of the fingers of one person to those of another.

In addition to the ordinary bluish-grey colour, red 89. and yellow have been observed to tinge Rays. The facts that their structure resembles that of the Inner 90.

89.
90.
Aura, and that they have never been observed to diminish the adjacent Outer Aura, either in density or brightness, justify the conclusion that the Rays and the Inner Aura have a common origin—the body, and that therefore a Ray is merely an extended bundle of striæ of the Inner Aura.

93.
96.
97.
98.
Dr. Kilner has found also that, under similar conditions, though with more difficulty, he was able to perceive a haze or Aura surrounding magnets, particularly the poles, having a bluish colour : a yellow Aura round a crystal of uranium nitrate ; a bluish Aura around the poles of galvanic cells, around any conductor joining the poles, and in the space between two wires connected each to one of the poles and to one another.

99.
From the facts (1) that the Inner Aura has a striated structure, whilst the Outer Aura is entirely nebulous ; (2) that the Inner Aura has a fairly well-marked border, that of the Outer Aura being ill-defined ; (3) that the outer margin of the Inner Aura is crenated, but that of the Outer Aura does not in any way correspond ; (4) that Rays proceed from the Inner Aura but in no case have been observed to commence in the Outer Aura and pass through to the Inner Aura—Dr. Kilner concludes (1) that the Outer Aura is most probably not derived from the Inner ; and (2) that the two Auras are most probably not the products of one and the same force.

101.
Dr. Kilner thus posits (1) No. 1 Auric Force (for short, 1AF), which originates the Inner Aura, and (2) No. 2 Auric Force (2AF), which originates the Outer Aura.

1AF acts apparently very intensely within a prescribed area. Through local increase of the force, rays may be projected consciously by an effort of will.

102.
2AF is more mobile and has a wider range of action than 1AF. It appears to be entirely independent of the will.

Different states of health, general or local, act on the forces, and through them on the Auras, though not necessarily in the same manner on both Inner and Outer Auras.

103.
A local affection may cause all the striæ to disappear

from the Inner Aura, the latter becoming more opaque and dense, and changing its colour ; it may also appear roughly rayed, in a manner quite different from the fine striæ of health ; or it may form a space devoid of the Inner Aura.

An affection over a large portion of the body may make the Inner Aura narrower on one side of the body than on the other ; this is accompanied by an alteration of texture in the Inner Aura and often also of colour.

Variations in the Outer Aura, consequent upon 2AF, 103. are less than is the case with the Inner Aura. The width may contract, but never quite disappear, and the colour may change. A change over a large area of the body may completely alter the shape of the Outer Aura. The Outer Aura may become narrower, the Inner Aura being unaffected ; but if the Inner shrinks, the Outer does so also.

Changes in the Auras may be produced by disease. 149. In hysteria, the Outer Aura is wider at the sides of the trunk : its width contracts suddenly near the pubes ; a bulge occurs at the back in the lumbar region.

In epilepsy, one side of both Inner and Outer Auras 158–160. for their whole length is usually contracted : the Inner 223. Aura becomes more opaque, the texture coarser, and striation diminishes or disappears. The colour is usually grey.

A contraction of the Inner Aura invariably implies a 223. grave malady. Occasionally an absolute break in the 227. Aura is observed.

The Inner Aura does not alter in shape or size to any 228. great extent, but it changes considerably in texture. The Outer Aura varies more frequently and more extensively in shape and size, but almost imperceptibly in texture.

In case of disease, the earliest morbid symptom is 221. diminution or complete loss of striation ; together with this, the granules become coarser, this being apparently due to amalgamation of smaller granules.

Derangement of the Inner Aura is accompanied by a 226. *pari passu* alteration of the Outer Aura.

228.   The preparation of the eye by means of the screens renders it difficult to appreciate accurately variations in the colour of the aura. The colour in the main appears to range from blue to grey, the colour depending more on temperament and mental powers than on 229.   changes in bodily health. The greater the mental vigour the bluer becomes the Aura ; deficiency of mental power tends to greyness in the Aura.

307   Dr. Kilner carried out a few experiments which demonstrated not only that Rays could be projected by an effort of will from various parts of the body, but also that the colour of a Ray or of a part of the Aura could 311.   be. varied by an effort of will. Red, yellow and blue 317.   colours have been produced in this way ; blue was found to be the easiest to produce, and yellow the most difficult.

A careful study of Dr. Kilner's results reveals that these agree with considerable accuracy with those obtained by clairvoyance. Dr. Kilner, however, appears to have studied more minutely, in some respects, the structure of the Aura and the effects on it of disease.

That which Dr. Kilner terms the Etheric Double is evidently identical with that which is described under the same name by clairvoyants. The striations of Dr. Kilner's Inner Aura are clearly the same as the Health Aura (see Chap. IV., p. 32). That which Dr. Kilner describes as the Outer Aura would appear to the present writer to consist of etheric particles from which the Prâna has been withdrawn and other etheric matter discharged from the body (see Chap. XI., Discharges). The student should compare the outlines of Auras given in Dr. Kilner's book with Plate XXIV. of the Health Aura in *Man, Visible and Invisible*.

It would appear legitimate to surmise that further improvement of Dr. Kilner's methods would lead to the physical perception of (1) the Etheric Chakrams ; (2) the flow of Prâna into and through the body ; (3) the nature and structure of the Etheric Double *within* the body. Dr. Kilner having referred to the difficulty of perceiving the Aura against a background of flesh, the present writer has wondered whether a suitable background could not be obtained by colouring in some way the skin of the person being observed.

Dr. Kilner states that his one objective in making his investigations has been to utilise the Aura as a means of diagnosis. It is, therefore, more than probable that further investigations would reveal properties of the Aura which, while perhaps having no diagnostic utility, would, nevertheless, be of scientific interest. 276.

From the observed facts—(1) that ill-health deranges the Aura ; (2) that the etheric matter of adjacent Auras flows together, forming Rays ; (3) that such Rays can be formed and directed by an effort of will ; (4) that the will can determine even the colour of such Rays— it would appear but a very short step to the subject of magnetic or mesmeric healing, and it is to be hoped that some investigator will make a study of this important and interesting subject in the same painstaking manner that has characterised Dr. Kilner's own researches.

CHAPTER XXII

ETHERIC FACULTIES

Cl 13.   ETHERIC faculties are extensions of the ordinary physical senses, enabling the possessor to appreciate " vibrations " pertaining to the etheric portion of the physical plane. Such impressions will be received through the retina of the eye, affecting of course its etheric matter.

Cl 14.   In some abnormal cases other parts of the etheric body may respond as readily as, or even more readily than, the eye. This would usually be due to partial astral development, the sensitive areas of the etheric double nearly always corresponding to the astral chakrams.

Cl 21.

Cl 22.   There are, roughly, two main kinds of clairvoyance, the lower and the higher. The lower variety appears sporadically in undeveloped people, such as savages of Central Africa, and is a sort of massive sensation vaguely belonging to the whole etheric body, rather than an exact and definite sense-perception communicated through a specialised organ. It is practically beyond the man's control. The Etheric Double being in exceedingly close relationship with the nervous system, any action on one of them reacts speedily on the other. In the lower clairvoyance the corresponding nervous disturbance is almost entirely in the sympathetic system.

Cl 22.   In more developed races the vague sensitiveness usually disappears as the mental faculties are developed. Later on, when the spiritual man begins to unfold, he regains clairvoyant power. This time, however, the faculty is precise and exact, under the control of the will, and exercised through a sense-organ. Any nervous action set up is almost exclusively in the cerebro-spinal system.

The lower forms of psychism are most frequent in *Cl* 22. animals and very unintelligent human beings. Hysterical and ill-regulated psychism is due to the small development of the brain and the dominance of the sympathetic system, the large nucleated ganglionic cells in this system containing a very large proportion of etheric matter, and thus being easily affected by the coarser astral vibrations.

Etheric vision may be temporarily stimulated, *e.g.*, *H S I I* 115. by delirium tremens, so that the sufferer may see etheric (as well as astral) creatures : the snakes and *Cl* 53. other horrors seen in such cases are almost invariably creatures of low type which feast on the alcoholic fumes exuding from the drunkard's body.

It should be noted that the Etheric Double is pecu- *M B* 29. liarly susceptible to the volatile constituents of alcohols.

Clairvoyant faculty may also sometimes be exhibited *Cl* 24, 52. under the influence of mesmerism ; also by an increased tenseness of the nerves, caused by excitement, hysteria, *T* 27 ; ill-health, drugs, or certain ceremonial rites which *M B* 55 ; *Cl* 52 ; induce self-hypnotisation. *T N P* 79.

It is not, however, advisable to allow oneself to be *I L I I* 194. thrown into mesmeric sleep in order to obtain clairvoyant experiences, because domination of the will by that of another person tends to make the will of the subject weaker and thus more liable to be acted upon by others.

Occasionally a person fortunate enough to have *H S I I* 323- gained the friendship of etheric nature-spirits may be 7. helped by these creatures to attain flashes of temporary clairvoyance, in order that the person may see them. In order to cultivate such friendship, it must be remembered that these nature-spirits are intensely shy and distrustful of men : they object to the physical emanations of the average man —of meat, tobacco, and alcohol ; also to low and selfish feelings, such as lust, anger, or depression. Strong, unselfish feelings of a lofty nature create the kind of atmosphere in which nature-spirits delight to bathe.

Almost all nature-spirits are fond of music, and some are especially attracted by certain melodies. Bishop Leadbeater writes that he has seen shepherd-boys in Sicily playing on their home-made Pan-pipe, with an appreciative audience of fairies frisking around them, of which they were probably blissfully unconscious. Sometimes, however, peasants do see the nature-spirits, as the literature of many peoples affirms.

M 123.

One method of developing etheric sight is by utilising the imagination. An endeavour is made to " imagine " what the inside of a physical object, such as a closed box, would be like, *i.e.*, to " guess," with an effort of strained attention, trying to see that which by ordinary sight could not be seen. After many attempts it is said that the " guessing " becomes more frequently correct than the theory of probability would demand, and presently the man begins actually to see etherically that which at first he only imagined. It is said that this practice is followed by the Zuni tribe of American Red Indians (see *Service Magazine*, April, 1925, article by Beatrice Wood).

N M 122–3; *S G O* 152.

Great numbers of people, if they will take the trouble to look, under suitable conditions of light, can see the mesmeric fluid, *i.e.*, the nerve-ether, as it streams from the hands of a mesmerist. Baron Reichenbach, in the middle of the nineteenth century, records that he found over sixty persons able to see these emanations, and some could see also a somewhat similar emanation pro-

R M 18; *T N P* 76.

ceeding from physical magnets, from crystals, and from a copper wire, one end of which was exposed to sunlight. The observers were usually shut up in a dark room for some hours in order to make the retina more sensitive.

T N P 77.

It is reported that some French scientists, who could not normally see the N Rays, became able to do so after sitting in darkness for three or four hours.

S C 144.

We may here note that N Rays are due to vibrations in the Etheric Double, causing waves in the surrounding ether. The student will recollect that N Rays are given off by animals, flowers and metals, but that all alike, when under the influence of chloroform, cease to emit them. They are also never emitted by a corpse. It will also be recollected that anæsthetics—such as chloroform—expel etheric matter from the physical body (see page 5), thus of course preventing the emanation of the Rays.

A full and controlled possession of etheric sight enables a man to see through physical matter : a brick wall, for example, seems to have the consistency of a light mist : the contents of a closed box could be accurately described and a sealed letter read : with a little practice it is also possible to find a passage in a closed book. *Cl* 30–1. *M* 29.

When the faculty is perfectly developed it is completely under control, and may be used or not used at will. It is said to be as easy to change from ordinary to etheric vision as to alter the focus of the eyes—the change being in reality a focussing of consciousness.

The earth is transparent to etheric vision to a certain extent, so that a man can see to a considerable depth, much as in fairly clear water. A creature burrowing underground could thus be seen, or a vein of coal or metal could be seen, if not too far below the surface. The medium through which we are looking is thus not perfectly transparent. *Cl* 32.

Bodies of men and animals are, in the main, transparent, so that the action of the internal organs can be seen, and to some extent disease may be diagnosed in this manner.

Etheric sight makes visible many entities, such as the lower orders of nature-spirits, which have etheric bodies : in this class are nearly all the fairies, gnomes and brownies, of which many stories are told in the highlands of Scotland, Ireland and other countries. *Cl* 32. *Cl* 33.

There is a class of beautiful fairies with etheric bodies who live upon the surface of the earth, and who have come up the ladder of evolution through grasses and cereals, ants and bees, and tiny nature-spirits. After their time as etheric fairies they become salamanders *H S I* 124.

or fire-spirits, then sylphs or air-spirits, and later still they pass into the kingdom of the angels.

H S I 130.   The forms of fairies are many and various, but most frequently human in shape and somewhat diminutive in size, usually with a grotesque exaggeration of some particular feature or limb. Etheric matter being plastic and readily moulded by the power of thought, they are able to assume almost any appearance at will, but, nevertheless, they have definite forms of their own which they wear when they have no special reason for taking any other.

H S I 152-3.   In order to take a form other than his own a fairy must conceive it clearly and keep his mind fixed upon it : as soon as his thought wanders he will at once resume his natural appearance.

Etheric matter does not obey the power of thought as instantaneously as does astral matter. We might say that mental matter changes *with* the thought, astral matter so quickly after that the ordinary observer can scarcely note any difference, but with etheric matter one's vision can follow the growth or diminution without difficulty. An astral sylph *flashes* from one shape to another ; an etheric fairy swells or decreases quickly, but *not* instantaneously.

H S I 152.   There are also limits, though wide ones, within which an etheric fairy can alter his size. Thus a fairy naturally 12 inches high might expand himself to 6 feet high, but only with a considerable strain which he could not maintain for more than a few minutes.

H S I 117-9.   One of the streams of evolving life, after leaving the mineral kingdom, instead of passing into the vegetable kingdom, assumes etheric vehicles, which inhabit the interior of the earth, living actually within solid rock, which offers no impediment to their motion or their vision. At a later stage, though still inhabiting the solid rock, they live close to the surface of the earth, and the more developed of them can occasionally detach themselves from it for a short time. These gnomes, which have sometimes been seen, and perhaps more frequently heard, in caves or mines, become visible either by materialising themselves by drawing around them a veil of physical matter, or, of course, by the spectator becoming temporarily etherically clairvoyant. They would be seen more frequently than they are, were it not for the rooted objection to the proximity of human beings which they share with all but the lowest types of nature-spirits.

Some of the lower types of etheric nature-spirits are not pleasing to the æsthetic sense. There are shapeless masses with huge red gaping mouths, which live upon the loathsome etheric emanations of blood and decaying flesh ; rapacious red-brown crustacean creatures which hover over houses of ill-fame ; and savage octopus-like monsters which gloat over the orgies of the drunkard and revel in the fumes of alcohol. *H S I* 128–9.

The entities posing or accepted as tribal deities, for whom blood sacrifices are made, or food, preferably of flesh, is burnt, are very low-grade creatures, possessing etheric bodies, for it is only through etheric bodies that they can absorb physical fumes and derive either nourishment or pleasure from them. *S G O* 217.

The stories told of ointments and drugs which, when applied to the eyes, enable a man to see fairy people have a basis of truth. No anointing of the eyes could open the astral vision, though, if rubbed over the whole body, some ointments assist the astral body to leave the physical in full consciousness. But the application to the physical eyes might easily stimulate etheric sight. *Cl* 34.

Etheric sight would of course make the Etheric Doubles of men visible : these doubles would often be seen hovering over newly-made graves : at séances etheric matter could be seen oozing from the left side of the medium, and one could perceive the various ways in which the communicating entities make use of it. *Cl* 35.

Etheric sight makes visible several entirely new colours, quite different from those in the spectrum, as we know it, and therefore indescribable in words we use at present. In some cases these other colours are combined with colours that we know, so that two surfaces which to ordinary eyes appear to match perfectly would appear different to etheric sight.

M 30.

For the chemist a whole fresh world would come under observation, and he could deal with ethers as he now deals with liquids or gases.

T B T 46, 193.

There are, belonging to the mineral kingdom, many etheric substances, the existence of which is unknown to Western science. Even the bodies of men, in the First Round, were constructed of etheric matter only, and resembled vague, drifting and almost shapeless clouds.

Etheric sight would inform us of the healthiness or otherwise of our surroundings, and we should be able to detect disease germs or other impurities.

H S I 110.

The beneficial effects of travel are partially due to the change of the etheric and astral influences connected with each place and district. Ocean, mountain, forest or waterfall—each has its own special type of life, astral and etheric as well as visible, and, therefore, its own special set of impressions and influences. Many of these unseen entities are pouring out vitality, and in any case the vibrations which they radiate awaken unaccustomed portions of men's Etheric Doubles, and of their astral and mental bodies, the effect being like that of exercising muscles which are not ordinarily called into activity—somewhat tiring at the time, yet distinctly healthy and desirable in the long run. Such amuse-

H S I I 122.

ments as rowing, for example, or swimming, especially in the sea, are of especial value, for the reasons named.

H S I 113.

There is a basis of truth in the tradition that it is strengthening to sleep under a pine tree with the head to the north, for the magnetic currents flowing over the surface of the earth, by steady gentle pressure, gradually comb out the entanglements and strengthen the particles both of the astral body and of the Etheric Double, and thus give rest and calm. The radiations of the pine tree make the man sensitive to the magnetic currents, and, in addition, the tree is constantly throwing off vitality in that special condition in which it is easiest for man to absorb it.

There is a kind of magnetic tide, an outflow and back-flow of magnetic energy between sun and earth, the turning points of which are at noon and midnight.

S O S 200.

The great etheric currents which are constantly sweeping over the surface of the earth from pole to pole possess a volume which makes their power as irresistible as that of the rising tide, and there are methods by which this stupendous force may be safely utilised, though unskilful attempts to control it would be fraught with great danger. It is also possible to use the tremendous force of etheric pressure.

S G O 200 ;
A P 112–3 ;
I L I 358.

In addition, by changing matter from a grosser to a subtler kind the vast store of potential energy which lies dormant may be liberated and utilised, somewhat as latent heat-energy may be liberated by a change of condition of visible matter.

A reversal of the above process enables one to change matter from the etheric to the solid condition, and thus to produce a " materialisation " phenomenon.

A P 115–6.

This faculty is sometimes employed in cases of emergency, where a man in his astral body, an " invisible helper," is in need of means of acting on physical matter. The faculty demands considerable power of sustained concentration, and the mind must not be taken off for one half-second, or the matter of the materialised form will instantly fly back into its original condition.

I H 41.

The reason why a physical object, after being reduced to the etheric condition, can afterwards be restored to its former shape, is that the elemental essence is retained in the same shape, and when the will-force is removed the essence acts as a mould round which the solidifying particles re-aggregate. If, however, a solid object be raised to a gaseous condition by heat, the elemental essence which informed the object would be dissipated —not because the essence itself can be affected by heat, but because when its temporary body is destroyed as a solid, it pours back into the great reservoir of such essence, much as a man's higher principles, though entirely unaffected by heat or cold, are yet forced out of a physical body when the latter is destroyed by fire.

Means may thus be employed to reduce a physical object to the etheric condition, and then to move it from one place to another, even through solid matter, such as a brick wall, by an astral current, with great rapidity. As soon as the disintegrating force is withdrawn, the matter is forced by the etheric pressure into its original condition.

Cl 36. When a man becomes etherically sensitive, in addition to sight, in most cases a corresponding change would at the same time take place in the other senses.

I L I 323. Thus it is claimed by astrologers that planetary influences, by expanding or congesting the etheric atmosphere, make the conditions for meditation respectively more or less favourable.

M W H W 374, 398. Incense is said to act on the etheric body somewhat as colours do on the astral body, and so may be employed to bring a man's vehicles rapidly into harmony. It appears that certain odours may be used to act on various parts of the brain.

The effect of etheric sight is quite different from that of astral sight. In the case of astral sight an entirely new element is introduced, often described as that of a

Cl 37. fourth dimension. With such vision, for example, a cube would be seen as though it were all flattened out, all its sides being equally visible as well as every particle within it.

Cl 38. With etheric sight, however, one merely sees *through* objects, and the thickness of matter through which one is looking makes a great difference to the clearness of the sight. Such considerations have no effect whatever on astral vision.

Cl 39. The word " throughth," used by W. T. Stead in referring to four-dimensional sight, is a perfect description, not of astral, but of etheric vision.

I L I I 202. Etheric sight can also be used for purposes of magnification. The method is to transfer impressions from the etheric matter of the retina direct to the etheric brain : the attention is focussed in one or more etheric particles, and thus is obtained a similarity of size between the organ employed and some minute object being observed.

A commoner method, though one demanding higher development, is to project a flexible tube of etheric matter from the centre of the chakram between the eyebrows, having one atom at its end which serves as a lens. Such an atom must have all its seven spirillæ fully developed. The atom can be expanded or contracted at will. This power belongs to the causal body, so that when an etheric atom forms the lens a system of reflecting counterparts must be introduced. *I L I I* 203. *I L I* 459.

By a further extension of the same power, the operator, by focussing his consciousness in the lens, can project it to distant points. *I L I I* 204.

The same power, by a different arrangement, can be used for diminishing purposes, this giving a vision of something too large to be taken in at once by ordinary vision.

This power was symbolised by a small snake projecting from the centre of the forehead in the head-dress of the Pharaoh of Egypt. *I L I* 459.

Much of the clairvoyance shown by dead people at a spiritualistic séance, enabling them to read passages out of a closed book, is of the etheric type. *S G O* 140.

One of the varieties of telepathy is etheric, and may take either of two forms. In the first an etheric image is made which can be seen by a clairvoyant; in the second the etheric waves, which the creation of the image generates, radiate out and, striking upon another etheric brain, tend to reproduce in it the same image. *S G O* 175.

The organ in the brain for thought-transference, both transmitting and receiving, is the pineal gland. If any one thinks intently on an idea, vibrations are set up in the ether which permeates the gland, thereby causing a magnetic current, which gives rise to a slight quiver or creeping feeling. This feeling indicates that the thought is clear and strong enough to be capable of transmission. With most people the pineal gland is not yet fully developed, as it will be in the course of evolution. *T N P* 99. *T P* 35.

I H 21-22. There is known to occult students a process by which rays of light may be bent, so that after passing round an object they may resume exactly their former course. This would, of course, make the object round which the rays were bent invisible to ordinary sight. It may be surmised that this phenomenon would result from a power to manipulate the particular form of etheric matter which is the medium for the transmission of light.

CHAPTER XXIII

MAGNETISATION OF OBJECTS

A MAN may employ his magnetism or vital fluid not only for mesmerising or healing other persons, but he may also use it to impregnate physical objects in a somewhat similar manner. Any object, in fact, which has been in close contact with an individual will absorb that individual's magnetism, and consequently will tend to reproduce in the person who wears it something of the same state of feeling or thought with which it is charged. This, of course, is part of the rationale of talismans, charms and relics, as well as of the feelings of devotion and reverential awe which sometimes quite literally exude from the walls of cathedrals and churches, each stone of which is a veritable talisman, charged with the reverence and devotion of the builder, consecrated by the bishop, and reinforced by the devotional thought-forms of successive generations for thousands of years. *S G O* 210. *S G O* 211. *S O S* 391-2.

The process is continually at work, though few are conscious of it. Thus, for example, food tends to become charged with the magnetism of those who handle or come near it, a fact which is at the back of the strict rules which Hindus observe regarding eating food in the presence of, or which has been subjected to the magnetism of, one of lower caste. To the occultist, magnetic purity is as important as physical cleanliness. Such foods as bread and pastry are especially liable to be charged with the magnetism of the person who prepares them, owing to the fact that magnetism flows out most strongly through the hands. Fortunately the action of fire in baking or cooking removes most kinds of physical magnetism. Some occult students, in order to prevent any avoidable mixture of magnetism, insist upon using only their own private eating utensils, and *H S I I* 3. *H S I I* 4. *H S I I* 5.

H S I I 28.　　even would not permit their hair to be cut except by some one of whose magnetism they approved, the head of course being the part of the body where alien magnetism would be most objectionable.

I L I I 199.　　Books, especially those in a public library, tend to become loaded with all kinds of mixed magnetism.

H S I I 67.　　Precious stones, being the highest development of the mineral kingdom, have very great power of receiving and retaining impressions. Many jewels are saturated with feelings of envy and greed and, in the case of some of the great historical jewels, are impregnated with physical and other emanations associated with crimes that have been committed in order to possess them. Such jewels retain these impressions unimpaired for thousands of years, so that psychometers may see around them pictures of indescribable horror. For this reason most occultists would discourage the wearing of jewels, as a general rule.

H S I I 67.
S G O 212.　　On the other hand, gems may be powerful reservoirs of good and desirable influence. Thus, for example, the Gnostic gems employed in Initiation ceremonies two thousand years ago retain even to this day powerful magnetic influence. Some Egyptian scarabœi are still effective, though much older even than the Gnostic gems.

H S I I 84.　　Money, in the form of coins and notes, is frequently charged with highly unpleasant magnetism. Not only does it become charged with a great mixture of different kinds of magnetism, but it is, in addition, surrounded by the thoughts and feelings of those who have handled it. The disturbing and irritating effect of such emanations on astral and mental bodies has been compared to that produced by the bombardment of radium emana-

H S I I 85.　　tions on the physical body. The worst offenders are copper and bronze coins, and old and dirty bank-notes. Nickel is less receptive of evil influences than copper, while silver and gold are better still in this respect.

　　Bedding affords another example of physical objects absorbing and emanating magnetic influence, many people having observed that unpleasant dreams may

often be caused by sleeping on a pillow which has been
used by a person of unpleasant character. If wool is
used for bedding or clothing, it is better not to let it
touch the skin, owing to it being saturated with animal
influences.

H S I I 92.

The method of deliberately manufacturing a talisman
is, first, thoroughly to cleanse the object of its present
etheric matter by passing it through a film of etheric
matter which has been created for the purpose by an
effort of will. The old etheric matter or magnetism
having been thus removed, the ordinary ether of the
surrounding atmosphere replaces it ; for there is an
etheric pressure somewhat corresponding to, though
immensely greater than, atmospheric pressure.

H S I I 206.

S G O 200 ;
A P 112.

A similar process is then effected for astral and
mental matter, the object thus becoming, as it were, a
clean sheet on which one may write as one wills. The
operator then, placing his right hand on the object,
fills himself with the particular qualities which he
wishes to convey to the talisman, and wills that those
qualities shall flow into it. An experienced occultist
can perform the whole process almost instantaneously
by a strong effort of will, but others will need to spend
more time on it.

The above would constitute one of the class of
General talismans. An *Adapted* talisman is one specially
charged to meet the requirements of a particular individual—almost like an individual prescription, rather
than a general tonic. An *Ensouled* talisman is one
designed to continue as a source of radiation for centuries. There are two varieties. In one there is placed
in the talisman a fragment of a higher mineral, which
throws out a ceaseless stream of particles. These particles become charged with the force stored in the talisman, the actual work of distribution being done by the
mineral, thereby greatly economising energy.

H S I I 212.

H S I I 213.

The second variety is one in which the ingredients
are so arranged as to make it a means of manifestation
of one of certain classes of undeveloped nature-spirits,
these latter providing the force necessary for the dis-

semination of the influence. Such talismans may last for thousands of years, to the intense delight of the nature-spirit and the great benefit of all who approach the magnetised centre.

H S I I 215.   A *Linked* talisman is one so magnetised as to bring it and keep it in close *rapport* with its maker, so that it becomes a kind of outpost of his consciousness. The wearer of the talisman could thus through his link send a cry for help to its builder, or the builder could direct a stream of influence through it to the wearer. Such a talisman would facilitate what Christian Scientists call " absent treatment."

H S I I 216.   In rare cases a physical talisman may be connected with the causal body of an Adept, as was done with those talismans buried in various countries by Apol-
I L I 32.   lonius of Tyana, about 1,900 years ago, in order that the force which they radiated might prepare those places to be the centres of great events in the future. Some of those centres have already been utilised, others are to be employed in the immediate future in connection with the work of the coming Christ.

I L I 205.   Great shrines are usually erected on the spot where some holy man lived, where some great event, such as an Initiation, took place, or where there is a relic of a great person. In any of these cases a powerful magnetic centre of influence has been created which will persist
S O S 403.   for thousands of years. Even if the " relic " does not happen to be a very powerful one, or is not even genuine, the centuries of devotional feeling poured out upon it by the hosts of visitors would make the place an active centre of beneficent radiation. The influence of all such places on visitors and pilgrims is unquestionably good.

It has already been mentioned that precious stones are naturally suited to be made into talismans or
H S I I 80.   amulets. The rudraksha berry, used frequently for necklaces in India, is eminently adapted for magnetisation where spiritual thought or meditation is required and disturbing influences are to be kept away. The beads made from the tulsi plant are another example,

though the influence they give is of a somewhat different character. An interesting set of natural talismans are those objects which produce strong scents. The gums of which incense is made, for example, can be chosen so as to be favourable to spiritual and devout thought. It is also possible so to combine ingredients as to produce the opposite effect, as was sometimes done by mediæval witches.

A trained occultist makes a regular practice of charging many things which pass from him to others with beneficent influences : such, for example, as letters, books, or presents. By a single effort of will he may charge even a typed letter far more effectively than it would be unconsciously charged when written by hand by some one not familiar with these truths. *H S I I 229.*

Similarly a trained occultist, by a mere wave of the hand, coupled with a strong thought, may almost instantaneously demagnetise food, clothing, bedding, rooms, etc. Such demagnetisation, while removing magnetism which has been externally impressed, would not affect the innate magnetism of objects, such, for example, as the inherently unpleasant vibrations of dead flesh, which even cooking could not destroy. *H S I I 5, 217.* *H S I I 7.*

The process of demagnetising rooms, etc., may be facilitated by the burning of incense or pastilles, or by sprinkling water, the incense and water being first passed through the process recommended for making talismans. *H S I I 218.*

It should also be borne in mind that as physical matter in man is in exceedingly close touch with the astral and mental, coarseness and grossness in the physical vehicle almost necessarily imply a corresponding condition in the other vehicles : hence the great importance to the occultist of physical as well as magnetic or etheric cleanliness. *H S I I 8.*

The " holy water " used in certain Christian churches affords a clear example of magnetisation, water being very readily charged with magnetism. The instructions given in the Roman rite make it quite evident that the priest is required, first, to " exorcise " the salt and *S G O 206.*

water, *i.e.*, to cleanse them from all objectionable influences, and then, making the sign of the cross, he is directed to " bless " the elements, *i.e.*, to pour his own magnetism into them, his will being directed to the purpose of driving away all evil thoughts and feelings.

S O S 397–8.   It is worth noting that salt contains chlorine, a " fiery " element, and hence the combination of water, the great solvent, with fire the great consumer, is highly effective as a cleansing agency.

S G O 209.   Precisely similar ideas underlie many other ceremonies in the Christian Church : such as baptism, in which the water is blessed and the sign of the cross made over it ; the consecration of churches and burial grounds, of the vessels of the altar, the vestments of the priests, bells, incense ; confirmation, the ordination of priests and consecration of bishops.

S O S 196.   In the Eucharist, the wine has a very powerful influence upon the higher astral levels, while the water sends out even etheric vibrations.

S O S 257.   At baptism, in the Liberal Catholic Church, the priest makes the sign of the cross over the forehead, throat, heart and solar plexus of the child. This has the effect of opening up these etheric chakrams, so that they grow to, perhaps, the size of a crown piece, and begin to sparkle and whirl as they do in grown-up people.

S O S 260.   In addition the magnetised water, as it touches the forehead, sets violently in vibration the etheric matter, stimulates the brain, and through the pituitary body affects the astral body, and through that the mental body.

S O S 263–4.   Later the priest, by anointing the top of the head with chrism, makes the chakram there serve as a kind of sieve, which rejects the coarser feelings, influences or particles, and also, by an effort of will, he closes the four centres which have been opened.

S O S 279.   At confirmation, the effect which has been produced on the âtmic principle is reflected into the Etheric Double.

S O S 343.   At the ordination of a priest, it is intended to clear the way between the higher principles and the physical brain. The blessing floods the etheric brain, and is meant to run up through the pituitary body, which is the point of closest junction between the dense physical, the etheric and the astral.

The anointing of the head of a bishop with chrism is intended so to act on the brahmarandra chakram that, instead of the usual saucer-like depression, it becomes more like a projecting cone, such as is often seen in statues of the Lord Buddha. *S O S* 361.

The ordination of the cleric is intended principally to act on the etheric body, that of the doorkeeper on the astral, that of the reader or lector on the mental, and that of the exorcist on the causal body. The exorcist is helped at his ordination to strengthen his power of healing. *S O S* 295-6.

There seems to have been an old custom—out of which has arisen the present Roman method of anointing the organs of the senses—of sealing all the chakrams in the body of a dying man, lest objectionable entities should seize upon that body as the owner left it and employ it for purposes of evil magic. *S O S* 382.

It is probable that many nervous affections could be helped by anointing with consecrated oil, and etheric disease might well be cured by means of " Unction." *S O S* 383.

In a Bishop's crozier, in the knob of which the consecrated jewels are placed, the etheric energy which radiates from the jewels is the outermost and the most prominent—so prominent in fact that it would not be surprising if physical cures could be effected by its touch. *S O S* 473-4.

Mediæval alchemists also employed somewhat similar methods in their use of magnetised swords, drugs, etc. *S G O* 204.

In the Ancient Mysteries, the thyrsus was a powerfully magnetised instrument, which was laid against the spinal cord of the candidate, giving him in that way some of the magnetism with which it was charged. *I L I* 130.

CHAPTER XXIV

ECTOPLASM

ECTOPLASM (from Greek ektos, outside, and plasma, mould, *i.e.*, that which is moulded *outside* the human body) is a name given to the matter, mainly if not wholly etheric, which exudes from a medium, and is employed for séance-room phenomena.

The late W. J. Crawford, D.Sc., in his books (*The Reality of Psychic Phenomena* (1916), *Experiments in Psychical Science* (1918), *Psychic Structures* (1921)) describes the painstaking and masterly researches he undertook into such phenomena as table-lifting, or "levitation," and rapping. For full details students are referred to those books, it being possible here to give a brief summary only of such results as are directly pertinent to our present study.

R P P 13, 238.

During all the experiments the medium was fully conscious.

W. J. Crawford approached the problems of table-lifting, etc., purely as problems in mechanics ; and, by means of force-registering appliances, both mechanical and electrical, he succeeded in discovering, by deduction from his observations, the *modus operandi* of the "psychic structures" employed. At a much later stage he was able completely to verify his deductions by direct vision and by photography, as will be explained in due course.

R P P 221-3.

Briefly, it was found that the ectoplasm, exuding from the medium, was prepared and shaped by the "operators" who control the production of the phenomena, into what he terms "rods." These rods or bars are attached at one end to the medium, and at the other, by suction, to table-legs or other objects, psychic force being then applied through the rods, and tables, etc., moved in various ways, without any purely physical contact with any person present. Raps and many other noises are produced by the rods striking on floor, table, a bell, etc.

By far the greater portion of the ectoplasm is usually obtained from the medium, though this is supplemented by a small portion from all, or most, of the other sitters present.

The ectoplasm can sometimes, even though quite invisible to ordinary sight, be felt. It is described as clammy, cold, reptilian, almost oily, as though the air *R P P* 146. were mixed with particles of dead and disagreeable matter.

The psychic rods issuing from the medium may vary *P S* 21, 25, 29 in diameter at their extremities from ½ inch to 7 or –30, 62–3 ; *E P S* 130. 8 inches, and the free end of each rod seems able to assume various shapes and degrees of hardness. The end may be flat or convex, circular or oval ; it may be soft as the flesh of a baby, or as hard as iron. The body of the rod feels solid a few inches from the free end, but then becomes intangible, though it resists, pulls, pushes, shear and torque.

In this intangible portion, nevertheless, a flow of *P S* 62–3 ; cold, spore-like particles can be felt, the flow being *R P P* 225 ; 219 ; outwards from the medium. There appears to be *E P S* 86–9. reason to believe that in some cases, though not in levitations, there is a complete circulation of etheric matter out from the medium and back to her again at a different part of the body. The condition of the end *P S* 25. of the rod as regards size and hardness can be varied on demand. The larger rods are usually fairly soft at the end, the smaller ones only becoming dense and hard.

W. J. Crawford considers it probable that the rods *R P P* 228–9. consist of a bundle of fine threads, intimately connected and adhering to one another. The psychic force passes along the threads, stiffening the whole structure into a rigid girder, which can then be moved as desired by forces applied within the body of the medium.

Certain experiments seem to indicate that the end *P S* 48. of a rod consists of a thick and more or less elastic film

P S 52.

or skin, stretched over a thin, somewhat serrated, elastic frame. The elasticity of the film is limited, and if too highly stressed the film may rupture, leaving the serrated frame exposed.

R P P 208–9.

The fact that an electroscope can be discharged by being touched by a rod indicates that the rod acts as a conductor of high tension electricity, discharging to earth through the medium's body to which it is attached.

E P S 83.

On the other hand, a rod placed across the terminals of a bell circuit does not cause the bell to ring, thus showing that it offers high resistance to low-tension current.

R P P 183.

White light usually destroys rod formations : even rays reflected from a surface on which psychic force is

P S 110–1.

exerted interfere with the phenomena. Red light, however, if not too strong, does not appear to injure the psychic structure, neither does light emanating from luminous paint which has been exposed for some hours to sunlight.

Usually the structures are quite invisible, though occasionally glimpses of them may be obtained. The

P S 10.

structures have been successfully photographed by flashlight, but great care must be taken not to injure

P S 149.

the medium. The shock to the medium when the flashlight impinges on the ectoplasm is much greater when the structure is under stress than when it is not stressed.

The large number of photographs taken confirm in every detail the conclusions arrived at by deduction from the phenomena themselves.

R P P 195.

The rigidity of a rod varies with the amount of light to which it is subjected, the hard end being, as it were, partially melted when exposed to light.

P S 1–4, 26–7.

In the case of objects being moved by psychic force there are two principal methods employed. In the first, one or more rods are projected from the medium, very frequently from the feet or ankles, sometimes from the lower part of the trunk, and are attached direct to the object to be moved, thus forming cantilevers. When tables are moved horizontally, the rods would usually be attached to the table-legs ; where they are lifted into the air, the rod or rods are often spread out

like a mushroom at the ends and attached to the under
surface of the table

In the second method the rod or rods projecting from
the medium are attached to the floor, and from the
point of attachment they are continued to the object
to be moved, thus forming no longer a cantilever but
something similar to a lever of the " First Order," the
Fulcrum being between the Weight and the Power.

Rods may be either straight or curved. They may
also be held suspended in the air in a rigid condition,
thus showing that they do not require to be pressing on
material bodies in order to remain rigid.

P S 16, 31.

In the case of the cantilever method, the whole of
the mechanical stress is transferred to the medium ; or,
more accurately, the greater portion to the medium,
and a much smaller portion to the other sitters. This
can be ascertained by ordinary mechanical appliances,
such as weighing machines and spring balances. If a
table is levitated, for example, by means of a cantilever, the weight of the medium will be increased by
about 95 per cent. of the weight of the table, and that
of the other sitters proportionately.

R P P 54, 56.

R P P 50, 154.

When, on the other hand, the rods are attached to
the floor, the weight of a levitated table is transmitted
direct to the floor, and the medium's weight, instead
of being increased, is *decreased*, the decrease being due
to the weight of the ectoplasm forming the rod, one end
of which rests on the floor.

When force is transmitted along a rod in order to
hold an object, such as a table, firmly to the floor, the
weight of the medium has been observed to be reduced
by as much as $35\frac{1}{2}$ lbs. On another occasion, when the
ectoplasmic structure was not stressed, the weight of
the medium has been reduced by $54\frac{1}{2}$ lbs., nearly half
the normal weight of the medium.

E P S 50-1.

E P S 78.

Cantilevers are usually employed to move or lift
light objects, but for heavy objects or for the transmission of great force, the rod or rods are attached
to the floor. Often a force approximating to a hundred-
weight is exerted.

E P S 101-3

R P P 14.

R P P 142.　　During levitation of objects the stress on the medium is often apparent in the stiffness, and even iron-like rigidity, of the muscles, principally of the arms, but also of the whole muscular system.　Later in his inves-

E P S 21.　tigations, however, W. J. Crawford found that the muscular rigidity had apparently entirely disappeared.

R P P 147–8;
E P S 126.　The production of these phenomena appears to result in a permanent loss of weight, both of medium and of sitters, but only to the extent of a few ounces. The sitters may lose more weight than the medium.

R P P 138,
140–1, 160,
225;
E P S 93.　As a rule, the placing of any material object within the space occupied by a rod, immediately breaks the line of communication, destroying the rod, as a rod.　A thin object, however, such as a pencil, may be passed through the vertical portion of a rod with impunity, but not through the portion between the medium and the table.　Interference with this portion may cause physical injury to the medium.

P S 5–6, 16;
E P S 33.　In order to make it possible for a rod to touch or adhere to, *e.g.*, a floor or table, the end of the rod has to be specially prepared, being made denser than the rest of the rod.　The process appears to be troublesome, or at least to consume time and force;　consequently the gripping portions of a structure are always kept to a minimum.

The method of gripping is by suction, as can easily be demonstrated by soft clay, referred to below.　Some-times the " suckers " can be heard slipping over the surface of wood, or taking new grips.

P S 82,
60–1.　Many instances, as well as photographs, are given by W. J. Crawford, of impressions on putty or soft clay, produced by the impact of rods.　These impressions are often covered with marks similar to the fabric of the medium's stockings.　The resemblance, however, is superficial, it being impossible to produce such impressions by actually pressing a stockinged foot on to the clay.　The impression made by the rod is much sharper than can be obtained by ordinary means, and is such as could be obtained if a fine viscous material were to cover the stocking fabric, to harden, and then to be pressed on the clay.

Further, the stocking marks may be greatly modified; *P S* 59-60.
the delicate pattern and tracery of the threads may be
distorted, thickened, partly covered over, or broken,
though still remaining recognisable as that of the
stocking fabric.

The deduction is that the ectoplasm is at first in a
state like that of a semi-liquid : that it oozes through
and round the holes in the fabric and partly sets on
the outside of the stocking. It is of a glutinous, fibrous
nature, and takes almost the exact form of the fabric.
It is then pulled off the stocking and built round the
end of the rod. For a large impression, the skin is
thickened and strengthened by the addition of more
materialising matter, and thus the original imprint
may be twisted, distorted, or partially obliterated.

Similarly, finger impressions may be made by a rod, *R P P* 204.
though these may be different in size from normal ones,
and may be much more clearly and regularly cut than
would be possible with ordinary finger impressions.

Raps, ranging from the slightest taps to blows of *R P P* 8-9,
sledge-hammer strength, as well as many other sounds, 183-4, 193.
are produced by semi-flexible rods, with suitably prepared ends, being struck against material objects. The
production of raps is accompanied by decrease of the
medium's weight, the amount of decrease, which may
be as much as 20 lbs. or more, being apparently directly *R P P* 198.
proportional to the intensity of the rap. The reason is
apparent : the rods being formed of matter from the
medium's body, the striking of such matter on the
floor, etc., necessarily transfers some of the medium's
total weight through the rod to the floor. The loss of
weight is temporary only, being restored when the
material of the rods returns to the medium.

The production of raps causes a mechanical reaction *R P P* 190-2,
on the medium, as though she were being pushed back- 196.
wards or struck. This reaction may cause her to make
slight involuntary motions with her feet. The stress on
the medium, however, is nothing like that caused by
levitation of objects.

Heavy blows, produced by a large rod, are not *R P P* 196-7;
P S 25.

usually delivered quickly. Light raps, however, usually produced by two or more thin rods, may be produced with incredible rapidity, the " operators " appearing to have great command over the rods.

R P P 149–50. In general, the production of these phenomena throws stress on all the sitters, as is apparent by spasmodic jerks, sometimes quite severe, which go round the whole circle previous to levitation. It would appear that the process of loosening and removing etheric matter from the bodies of the sitters takes place in jerks, and, to some extent, affects them all together.

R P P 238–9. W. J. Crawford reports that an entity, purporting to have been whilst alive a medical man, and to speak through the medium (on this occasion entranced for the purpose), stated that there are two kinds of substance used in the production of phenomena. One is taken in comparatively large quantities from medium and sitters, all, or nearly all, being returned to them at the close of the séance. The other can be obtained only from the medium, and, as it consists of the most vital material from the interior of her nerve-cells, it can be taken only in minute quantities without injury to the medium. Its structure is broken up by the phenomena, and therefore it cannot be returned to the medium. This statement has not been verified or confirmed in any way and is given purely on its merits.

P S 127. W. J. Crawford devised and used with great success the " staining method " of tracing the movements of ectoplasm. Ectoplasm possessing the property of adhering strongly to such a substance as powdered carmine, the latter is placed in its path, when a coloured track will be found. By this means it was discovered

P S 137–8. that ectoplasm issues from and returns to the lower part of the trunk of the medium. It has considerable consistency, for it has a strong tearing action on the stock-

P S 80. ings or other clothing and will sometimes pull out whole threads, several inches long, from a stocking, carry, and deposit the same in a vessel of clay placed some distance from the medium's feet.

P S 92. The ectoplasm follows a path down the legs and

enters the shoes, passing between stocking and shoe, wherever there is space. If it has picked up dye on its way it will deposit this at any place where foot, stocking and shoe are in close contact, *i.e.*, where there is not sufficient room for it to pass.

The solidification, as well as the dematerialisation, *P S* 78. of the hard end of a rod is effected immediately the rod issues from the medium's body. For this reason, the free end of a rod, unless it be one of the thinnest, cannot *E P S* 94-7. penetrate closely woven cloth, or even wire netting of 1-inch mesh, if placed more than an inch or two in front of the medium. If such screens, however, are very close to the medium's body, an imperfect materia- *E P S* 128. lisation of the end of the rod may take place and limited psychic phenomena may occur.

The evolution of ectoplasm from the body of a *P S* 146-7. medium is accompanied by strong muscular movements all over the body, and the fleshy parts of the body, especially from the waist downwards, become reduced in size, as though the flesh had caved in.

W. J. Crawford is convinced that in the production *P S* 19-20. of séance-room phenomena there are at least two substances employed : (1) a component, forming the basic part of the psychic structure, which is invisible, impalpable, and generally outside the range of physical things altogether, and (2) a whitish, translucent, nebulous substance, mixed with (1) in order to enable (1) to act on physical matter; (2), he considers, is in all probability identical with the material used in materialisation phenomena.

Many phenomena of materialisation are described, with that scrupulous and minute attention to detail so characteristic of German investigators, in a large work entitled *Phenomena of Materialisation*, by Baron von Schrenck Notzing (1913), and translated by E. E. Fournier d'Albe, D.Sc. (1920).

In addition to elaborate descriptions of large numbers of séances and phenomena, there are given some 200 photographs of materialised forms, or apparitions of many kinds, ranging from threads or masses of ecto-

K

plasm to fully-formed faces. The main conclusions may be epitomised as follows. These are taken largely, for convenience, from a lecture on " Supra-Normal Physiology and the Phenomena of Ideoplastics," by Dr. Gustave Geley, a Paris psychologist and physician, which is printed at the end of Baron Notzing's book.

P M 328–32, 322.

From the body of the medium there emanates a substance which at first is amorphous or polymorphous. It may appear as ductile dough, a true protoplasmic mass, a kind of shaking jelly, simple lumps, thin threads, cords, narrow rigid rays, a broad band, a membrane, fabric, woven material or net with fringes and rucks.

P M 76 (*footnote*), 98, 111.

The thread- or fibre-like nature of the substance has frequently been observed.

It may be white, black or grey, sometimes all three appearing together : white is perhaps the most frequent. It appears to be luminous.

P M 95, 227, 323.

P M 58, 98.

Usually it seems to be odourless, though sometimes it may have a peculiar smell, impossible to describe.

P M 108, 112, 111, 118, 234, 276.

There seems no doubt that it is subject to the influence of gravity.

P M 329–32, 276, 324.

To the touch it may be moist and cold, viscous and sticky, more rarely dry and hard. When expanded it is soft and slightly elastic, when formed as cords it is hard, knotty and fibrous. It may feel like a spider's web passing over the hand : the threads are both rigid and elastic. It is mobile, with a creeping, reptilian motion, though sometimes it moves suddenly and quickly. A draught may set it in motion. Touching it produces a painful reaction on the medium. It is extremely sensitive and appears and disappears with lightning rapidity. It is usually sensitive to light, though sometimes the phenomena will withstand full daylight. Flashlight photographs of it can be taken, though the flash acts like a sudden blow on the medium.

P M 53.

P M 21, 322.

During the production of the phenomena the cabinet, containing the medium, is usually in darkness, but the curtains are frequently drawn aside, and outside the cabinet red light is used, and sometimes even white light up to 100 candle-power.

The substance has an irresistible tendency towards organisation. It assumes many forms, sometimes indefinite and non-organised, but most frequently organic. Fingers, including nails, all perfectly modelled, complete hands, faces, and other shapes may be formed.

The substance emanates from the whole body of the medium, but especially from the natural orifices and extremities, from the top of the head, the breasts, and the finger-tips. The most usual origin, and most easily observed, is the mouth, the inner surface of the cheeks, the gums and the roof. *P M 329, 59.*

The materialised forms have a certain independence, a hand, for example, being able to move its fingers and grasp the hand of an observer, though sometimes the human skin seems to repel the phantoms. The structures are sometimes smaller than in nature, being really miniatures. The back of the materialisations has been observed to be without organic form, being merely a mass of amorphous substance, the forms containing a minimum of substance necessary to make them appear real. The forms may disappear very gradually, fading away, or almost instantaneously. During the whole time it is clear that the forms are in physiological and psychical connection with the medium, the sensation reflex of the structures coalescing with that of the medium. Thus, a pin inserted into the substance would cause pain to the medium. *P M 96, 160.* *P M 6, 283.* *P M 99.*

It seems that the substance can be influenced both by the general direction and the subject-matter of the thoughts of the sitters. In addition the medium, usually in the hypnotic state, is exceedingly open to the influence of suggestion. *P M 22, 151.*

Pieces of the materialised forms have been seized in a porcelain dish and retained. On one occasion, when examined afterwards, two pieces of skin were found which, under the microscope, were recognised as human. On another occasion 3 or 4 c.c. of a transparent liquid, *P M 75.* *P M 113.*

P M 117.

P M 247.

without air bubbles, were found. Analysis revealed a colourless, slightly turbid, non-viscous, odourless liquid, slightly alkaline, with a whitish precipitate. The microscope disclosed the components of cell detritus and saliva, the substance evidently originating from the mouth. On yet another occasion a bundle of fair hair, not in any way resembling the darker hair of the medium, was found, the hand of the observer being covered with mucus and moisture. In addition, fragments of other substances are sometimes found, such as face-powder or shreds of the medium's clothing.

CHAPTER XXV

CONCLUSION

CONSIDERABLE as is the total of information at present available regarding man's etheric body and etheric phenomena in general, nevertheless the serious student will at once perceive that the field for future research is vastly greater than the fragments of it which have so far been explored.

In view of the intimate bearing which the structure, nourishment and health of the etheric body have on physical health, and on the functioning, not only of the physical body, but also of the other bodies in their connection with the physical, it is abundantly evident that research into every class of etheric phenomena should lead to discoveries of great scientific interest and beneficent import to man.

A number of methods of conducting such research is open to us. First, we have the method of direct clairvoyant observation, at different levels, it being probable, in view of the rapid development of certain sections of the human race at the present time, that large numbers of persons will find themselves, in the not distant future, in possession of etheric faculties.

In addition to etheric faculties, normally unfolded in the ordinary course of evolution, Dr. Kilner's line of work appears to indicate that these faculties may be stimulated by the use of screens, such as he employed, and possibly by other physical means yet to be devised. Both mesmerism and hypnotism might also, with adequate safeguards, be employed to make available latent etheric faculty. The use of photography may in the future become very extensive and important, the salts used in the photographic plate being sensitive to wave-lengths and degrees of light beyond the reach

of the normal eye. A further method of research, using
ultra-violet light, also offers great promise. A laboratory for this purpose has recently been opened at Leeds,
through the initiative and far-seeing enterprise of some
members of the Theosophical Society in that town.

The methods employed by W. J. Crawford may well
be pursued by other workers, and additions thus be
made to the exceedingly valuable results obtained by
the able investigator named.

As to the desirability of utilising the séance-room for
obtaining such materialisation phenomena as those
obtained, *e.g.*, by Baron von Notzing, there is likely to
be divergence of opinion. It is fairly generally admitted
that phenomena of this nature may easily be highly
injurious to the medium, both physically and in other
ways, and there is also something distinctly unsavoury
about the materialisations produced by these means.
On the other hand, it may be urged that if mediums are
willing to sacrifice themselves in the cause of science,
science is justified in accepting such sacrifices ; and,
further, that science as such has no concern with the
savouriness, or otherwise, of natural phenomena. It
seems fairly certain, however, that the highest spiritual
teachers of the present day do not look with favour on
the séance-room. Yet it may be argued that in other
ages the use of vestal virgins, soothsayers, " prophets,"
and other mediums, received the sanction and approval
of high authorities. The present writer, therefore,
refrains from offering any dogmatic conclusion on this
point.

The possibility of utilising knowledge of etheric
phenomena for purposes of healing would appear to be
almost limitless. For many cases of disease, physical,
emotional or mental, the employment of vital or
magnetic healing, and also mesmerism and hypnotism,
would seem to be in line with the general progress of
thought in this direction. In particular, the use of
mesmerism to produce anæsthesia for surgical or other
purposes, in place of ether, gas, or chloroform, would
appear to possess many recommendations.

It may also be surmised that the science of Osteo-
pathy, in conjunction with the study of the force-
centres and the flow of vitality in the human body,
should lead to valuable results.

The remarkable discoveries of Dr. Abrams, which
appear to have been accepted, at least partially, by the
medical profession, would seem to be capable of con-
ferring almost incalculable benefit on the disease-
ridden human race of to-day. Although it is not, the
present writer believes, rigidly proved, yet it would
appear to be almost certain that the methods employed
in the Abrams system act, directly or indirectly, on
and through the etheric body.

The recent revival of healing by various Christian
Churches would also seem to have a great future, and
there can be little doubt that such methods, while far
from being wholly physical, yet do work, to some
extent, through etheric matter.

The possibility of utilising our knowledge of etheric
phenomena extends, however, even further afield than
is roughly indicated above. Thus it seems more than
probable that an important, and hitherto almost un-
recognised, factor in the treatment of disease and the
preservation of health would derive from the etheric,
apart from the purely physical properties of drugs,
waters, gases, the air, emanations of soils and minerals,
fruit, flowers and trees. It is possible in the future that
we may discover health resorts, either on land, lake or
sea, which depend for their curative powers on their
etheric properties.

The attention which has recently been devoted to
the wider use of sunlight obviously has a close bearing
on what we know concerning the emanations of Prâna
from the sun, its diffusion in the atmosphere, and its
absorption by living beings.

It may be that further knowledge of etheric and vital
phenomena may lead to a profound change of attitude
towards the use in medicine and dietetics of substances
which have passed through, or are derived from, animal
organisms.

It is a reasonable conjecture that those elusive substances known as vitamins may owe their beneficent properties to the presence in them, in one form or another, or Prâna, or possibly to the quality of the etheric matter they contain.

A recognition of the fact that the vitality of the body is derived, not from food, but direct from the atmosphere, may well lead to a radical change in the dietetic treatment of sick persons, and also to a much greater use of fasting as a curative agency. Those who are familiar with the literature of fasting will no doubt be aware that several writers on this interesting subject have already deduced from actual observation that the connection between the assimilation of food and the acquirement of vital energy is very far from being simple or direct.

It is now generally recognised that the use of electricity for curative purposes has not fulfilled all that was at first hoped for it. It may be that a deeper knowledge of etheric phenomena will be of assistance in devising better methods of utilising electricity for curative purposes : the association of electricity with etheric matter (of which the Etheric Double is composed) is a phenomenon which may thus be turned to valuable account.

In fact, it would scarcely be too much to say, that in the future the etheric body, being the habitat, so to say, of the life-principle in its physical aspect, may receive as much attention as, or even more than, is now given to the material physical body. The utilisation, eventually, of energy associated with the physical ether, for many purposes, is obvious, and needs no insistence here. The student of occultism, however, will recollect the warning that men will not be permitted to release the almost incalculable forces latent in atomic matter until it is assured that such forces will be used beneficently, and not for purposes of destruction, as has unfortunately happened in the case of so many scientific discoveries in the past.

It is further evident that the discovery of the etheric

grades of matter will open up new vistas in chemistry and physics, and may even be turned to useful account in the production of food substances of all kinds, of electrical conductors or insulators, materials for clothing, and many other substances used in daily life.

Finally, both on its own intrinsic account and also as a stepping-stone to knowledge of even higher things, a recognition by orthodox scientists of the existence of the etheric body, and a study of its constitution and behaviour—both of which we venture to think cannot now be long delayed—may prove a firm foundation on which may be raised a vast superstructure of knowledge of ultra-physical things. For (to adapt and abridge the closing paragraphs of *The Idyll of the White Lotus*), that which is to come is grander, more majestically mysterious, than the past. By slow and imperceptible progress, the teachers of men drink their life from purer sources, and take their message more directly from the soul of existence. Life has in it more than the imagination of men can conceive. The real blossom of life grows above the stature of man, and its bulb drinks deep from the river of life. In the heart of that flower man will read the secrets of the controlling forces of the physical plane, and will see, written within it, the science of mystic strength. He will learn how to expound spiritual truths, and to enter into the life of his highest self, and he can learn also how to hold within him the glory of that higher self, and yet to retain life upon this planet so long as it shall last, if need be ; to retain life in the vigour of manhood, till his entire work is completed, and he has taught to all who look for light these three truths :—

The soul of man is immortal, and its future is the future of a thing whose growth and splendour has no limit.

The principle which gives life is in us and without us, is undying and eternally beneficent, is not heard or seen or smelt, but is perceived by the man who desires perception.

Each man is his own absolute lawgiver, the dispenser

of glory or gloom to himself ; the decreer of his life, his reward, his punishment.

These truths, which are as great as life itself, are as simple as the simplest mind of man. Let the food of knowledge be given to all those who are hungry for it.

INDEX